TWO MINUTES
IN THE **BIBLE**™

FOR
Women

SHANA SCHUTTE
WITH **BOYD BAILEY**

HARVEST HOUSE PUBLISHERS
EUGENE, OREGON

Cover by Left Coast Design

Cover Photo © Glass and Nature / Shutterstock

TWO MINUTES IN THE BIBLE is a trademark of Boyd Bailey. Harvest House Publishers, Inc., is the exclusive licensee of the trademark TWO MINUTES IN THE BIBLE.

TWO MINUTES IN THE BIBLE™ FOR WOMEN
Copyright © 2017 Boyd Bailey
Published by Harvest House Publishers
Eugene, Oregon 97402
www.harvesthousepublishers.com

ISBN 978-0-7369-6786-0 (pbk.)
ISBN 978-0-7369-6787-7 (eBook)

Library of Congress Cataloging-in-Publication Data
Names: Schutte, Shana, 1967- author. | Bailey, Boyd, 1960- author.
Title: Two minutes in the Bible for women / Shana Schutte with Boyd Bailey.
Description: Eugene, Oregon : Harvest House Publishers, 2017.
Identifiers: LCCN 2016030263 (print) | LCCN 2016032719 (ebook) | ISBN
    9780736967860 (pbk.) | ISBN 9780736967877 ()
Subjects: LCSH: Christian women—Religious life. | Christian women—Prayers
    and devotions. | Bible—Meditations.
Classification: LCC BV4527 .S2787 2017 (print) | LCC BV4527 (ebook) | DDC
    242/.643—dc23
LC record available at https://lccn.loc.gov/2016030263

Printed in the United States of America

16 17 18 19 20 21 22 23 24 / BP-SK / 10 9 8 7 6 5 4 3 2 1

To my wonderful husband, Clark.
Every day is a blessing being married to you,
and every day I am so grateful the Lord brought us together.
Thank you for loving me.
I am a rich woman because I have you in my life.

Acknowledgments

Life is full of surprises. The great thing is that along with the challenges we didn't expect, there are blessings that catch us unaware and fill us with thankfulness. Such was the opportunity to write this book. Thank you for thinking of me, Boyd Bailey, and asking me to partner with you on this project. It has been an honor. I hope we can do it again!

I am also grateful for the talented people who edited my words and smoothed out my mistakes. Thanks to Susan Fox at Wisdom Hunters, Jean Bloom of Bloom in Words Editorial Services, and the team at Harvest House, including Betty Fletcher, Steve Miller, and Steve Kuhn.

And most importantly, thank you to my Lord Jesus Christ. I am in awe of Your grace and love.

A Note from the Author

I married late in life. Late as in several of my high school classmates were already grandparents. Late as in I had been coloring my hair for ten years, and late as in I had just found my first gray eyebrow hair. Yep! It was late.

Right after my engagement, I felt stretched beyond my comfort zone as I prepared to transition from being Shana the single, Shana the writer, and Shana with the family from Southern Idaho to Shana the wife and stepmom to five fabulous grown children and two sons-in-law.

Now, two years after saying "I do," there are still some days when I feel stretched beyond my comfort zone, days when I am forced to press into Christ out of desperation. At these times, I need to experience His sufficiency. I need Him to be my Enough.

I have needed Christ to be my Enough as I have wrestled with the normal insecurities that come with becoming a part of a blended family. I have needed Him to be my Enough as I have moved from "I still show up to family holiday gatherings without bringing a dish since I am unmarried" to "I am the Thanksgiving chef in this family" even though—up until the time my husband and I tied the knot—I had never made a turkey or even purchased a can of cranberry sauce. In so many ways I have needed Him to be my Enough.

But the need to experience Christ's sufficiency hasn't just been a marriage thing. It's been a *life thing*. I needed Christ to be my Enough during my single days when I was alone and lonely. I needed Him to be my Enough as I prayed through tear-filled nights, friendship failures, ruined romances, money messes, and dashed dreams. In fact, there hasn't been a moment in my entire life when I haven't needed Him. I have always needed Him to be my sufficiency, and I am so grateful that He always has been—even during those times when I thought He wasn't.

I don't share my story because it's all that interesting or unusual. Rather, I share it because it's *so typical.* It's so typical of God to be so good because *He is* goodness. It's so typical of Him to be so loving because *He is* love. It's so typical of Him to be so faithful in demonstrating His sufficiency, because that's what He *is.* He *is* our Sufficiency.

I wrote some of the devotionals in this book while I was still flying solo and some later after my husband and I married. While my story changed, God's story never has. He is the same yesterday, today, and forever (Hebrews 13:8). His love never fails (Psalm 136). He is always Enough.

You may feel as if God can't possibly be your Enough because you are in a very difficult place on your journey. Maybe you are unhappily single, unhappily married, or unhappily divorced. You are shy, unemployed, or in a financial fix. You feel rejected, unwanted, overlooked, unseen, unimportant, or like you are without purpose. Let me encourage you: Jesus is Enough for anything you are experiencing. He wants to be your sufficiency, and He died on the cross to prove it. Since He has given us such a great and precious gift, won't He also give us all things (Romans 8:32)?

As you read each daily message, which was inspired by Jesus teaching me that He is my Enough, I pray that you will also come to know that He is your Enough too, no matter what you are going through.

Grow complete in God's love,
Shana

1

The Power of Gratitude over Grief

*Give thanks to the L*ORD*, for he is good;*
his love endures forever.

Psalm 107:1

Because I was just around the corner from age 46 when I said "I do," I grieved the death of my fairy-tale family. The chance of having babies was next to nil, and even though I was submitted to God's plan, I still experienced a season of grief-filled tears. One afternoon I visited a Christian counselor. I shared my story with her and then asked, "How do I keep from getting stuck in grief?"

She said one word that has stayed with me: "Gratitude."

Ah, yes. Gratitude. Gratitude enables us to see past the fog of our current circumstances to raise our gaze from the here and now to eternity. And practicing gratitude isn't just good because it makes you feel warm and fuzzy. It's not even good because it's a distinguishing mark of a faithful Christ follower. Gratitude can literally be the difference between internal life and death, between thriving in life as Christ promises we can and just surviving.

∽

"I have come that they may have life,
and have it to the full" (John 10:10).

But practicing gratitude doesn't mean you have to deny the pain of your losses and say "I'm so glad my story turned out like it did." It also doesn't mean you have to say you are glad bad things happened. But it does mean you make peace with what happened. It means you are able to say, "Lord, I may not have chosen this path, but I trust You, and I know I am never out of Your loving hands. I believe You are working everything out for my good and Your glory, and I surrender to You." Living with a grateful heart means you accept God is sovereignly weaving your story together even when it involves loss.

Then, when you choose gratitude, you can look to the future in hope. Rather than asking, "Why did this happen to me?" you can ask, "Lord, what do You want to do with my life now?" That's the power of gratitude. It's redemptive, powerful, and life-changing.

∽

> "The Lord has done it this very day; let us
> rejoice today and be glad" (Psalm 118:24).

How can you actively practice gratitude today despite your losses?

Related Readings
Psalm 34:18; Colossians 3:17; Revelation 21:4

2

Freedom from Carrying Your Own Burdens

I will not leave you as orphans;
I will come to you.

John 14:18

I n some seasons in my life, as perhaps you have in yours, I have tried to carry the weight of life alone. During one of these seasons, the Lord ministered to me about trusting Him rather than living like a spiritual orphan, and resting in His love rather than striving. One afternoon, I had my pen and notebook in hand when the following thoughts came to mind. They are written as if God is speaking. If you wrestle with striving, if you have a difficult time believing the Lord will provide for you, or if you live like a spiritual orphan, I hope these words are an encouragement.

The daughter who has forgotten she is fathered, that she has an Abba who loves her, will try to live independently of Me because she isn't sure I am with her; she isn't convinced I will take care of her. So she strives and works and strives and works like an orphan who must take care of herself. She acts like she has no Father while she confesses that she knows Me. Indeed, she is Mine, but she isn't allowing Me to parent her the way a good father does. Instead, she tries to carry the weight of her life and her responsibilities all on her own. She has forgotten that true rest is found in belief and faith.

✂

"And to whom did God swear that they would
never enter his rest, if not to those who disobeyed?
So we see that they were not able to enter,
because of their unbelief" (Hebrews 3:18-19).

The woman who does not trust cannot rest even if she wants to, because she is always driven, out of her unbelief, to self-protection and striving. "I will do it myself!" But the dependent child brings everything to her daddy. She brings her worries. She brings her responsibilities. She brings her fears, financial needs, and friendships. She brings her love life and loneliness. She brings her marriage, her money, and her mate. She brings Me her life.

She lays down all the pieces of her existence at My feet, day after day. She brings whatever burdens she is carrying and she unloads them all to Me. She knows she is loved, and she can rest because there is rest in love.

✂

"Come to me, all you who are weary and burdened,
and I will give you rest" (Matthew 11:28).

What do you fear will happen if you let go and let God parent you the way a good father does?

Related Readings
Psalms 68:5; 91:1-16; Isaiah 64:8

3

Is Love Really All You Need?

Let him kiss me with the kisses of his mouth—
for your love is more delightful than wine.

Song of Songs 1:2

In 1967, the Beatles released a recording called "All You Need Is Love," a song initially performed on the world's first global television link. The Beatles manager, Brian Epstein, said of the song, "The nice thing about it is that it cannot be misinterpreted. It is a clear message saying that love is everything."

A lot in the world has changed since 1967, but one thing hasn't changed: our culture is still sending out the message that love—particularly romantic love—is all you need. Movies, radio, and magazines tell us that if we can just find our soul mate, all our problems will disappear. While love is from God, there are limitations to earthly love, regardless of how wonderful another person may be. Therefore, adjusting our unrealistic expectations about love can be one of the best things we can do. When we realize only God can love us completely, it makes all the difference between being joyful or miserable in our relationships.

❦

"But the fruit of the Spirit is...peace" (Galatians 5:22).

In his book *Counterfeit Gods*, Timothy Keller writes, "Putting the weight of all your deepest hopes and longings on the person you are

marrying, you are going to crush him or her with your expectations...
No person, not even the best one, can give your soul all it needs." Keller
also writes, "We maintain the fantasy that if we find our one true
soul mate, everything wrong with us will be healed. But when our
expectations and hopes reach that magnitude, as [Ernest] Becker says,
'the object of love is God.' No lover, no human being is qualified for
that role. No one can live up to that. The inevitable result is bitter
disillusionment."[1]

If disillusionment becomes a part of our stories, bitterness of heart
may not be far behind. We may give up on love as our expectations
betray us. We will close our hearts off to others because we believe love
always disappoints. To be free from unrealistic expectations about love,
we must continually press into God for our needs, reject the lies of our
culture, practice gentle grace in our relationships, remember we are not
perfect, and keep our eyes firmly fixed on Christ. We must also remember God created us for relationships; we were not created to worship
relationships.

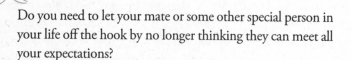

"You shall have no other gods before me" (Exodus 20:3).

Do you need to let your mate or some other special person in
your life off the hook by no longer thinking they can meet all
your expectations?

Related Readings
Luke 6:31; Romans 12:9; 1 Corinthians 13:4-8

4

How to Bless Someone You Can't Have a Relationship With

Love your enemies and pray for those who persecute you.

Matthew 5:44

As part of my goal to discover what Scripture teaches about true forgiveness, I once read Luke 6:28, where Jesus says, "Bless those who curse you, pray for those who mistreat you." I looked up the word "bless" in my *Complete Word Study New Testament* and discovered its meaning sounds a lot like our word "eulogy." It means "to speak well of someone, to express good wishes."[2] Therefore, when we bless someone, we speak well of them and express good wishes. And our verbal blessings for even our enemies are a sign true forgiveness has taken place in our hearts.

As part of my study, I also discovered that when God blesses us, His blessing is always coupled with action. Unlike people, He doesn't say one thing but then do something else. His blessings and actions are always in agreement. Therefore, if we want to be like God, we bless with our mouths *and* with our actions.

〜

"Bless those who persecute you;
bless and do not curse" (Romans 12:14).

But what about when a relationship doesn't allow us to associate with someone? How can we bless them in action? What if we need to apply firm boundaries but still want to follow Luke 6:28? The wonderful news is that when we can't bless someone verbally and with our actions, we can bless them through prayer. We can express good wishes to God on their behalf and ask Him to follow up with the action of blessing.

I did this one morning as I prayed for someone to whom I needed to apply Luke 6:28. I asked God to bless her in action as I blessed her with my words in prayer. "O Lord, I pray You will bless her coming in and going out. Bless her lying down and her rising up. Bless her relationships and her work. Provide for her, prosper her, and help her to know You more."

We are called to bless, not to curse. And when we are unable to bless others through action (the way God does), we speak blessings through prayer and ask God to follow up by blessing them in action.

‡

"If you love those who love you, what
reward will you get? Are not even the tax
collectors doing that?" (Matthew 5:46).

Do you need to bless someone through prayer today?

Related Readings
Matthew 5:46; Romans 12:14-21; 1 Corinthians 13:4-8; James 4:17

5

Is It Time to Let Go?

To everything there is a season,
a time for every purpose under heaven.

Ecclesiastes 3:1 NKJV

The writer of Ecclesiastes follows the verse above with a list of seasons, or "times," such as birth and death, weeping and laughing, and mourning and dancing. He even includes "a time to plant and a time to pluck what is planted."

I don't know about you, but I usually don't enjoy plucking up anything that was planted by either me or God. First of all, it takes time, and second, it can be painful to pluck. You know what I mean. You have a relationship or friendship God is asking you to relinquish. Sure, He planted it in a past season of your life, and it served its purpose. But now He is asking you to uproot it because He wants to do something different. Or perhaps God is saying about your job, "Let it go. I want to uproot it. I've got a new purpose planned for you." Oh, but we're so slow to let go because it can be painful, inconvenient, and sometimes just plain hard work! But what do we forfeit if we insist on holding on to the old things that either we or God planted in old seasons?

Blessed are those who hear the word of
God and observe it" (Luke 11:28 NASB).

When we refuse to let go, we forfeit our effectiveness for Him. We forfeit the peace of knowing we are following Christ no matter what. Thankfully, we can rest assured of one thing: God never asks us to uproot anything in our lives without a reason and a plan. He always asks because He wants to plant some kind of new seed to bring about a good change.

Are you afraid to pluck up something even though its season in your life is over? Yes, you can be sure moving into the unknown with God will never be comfortable, but it will always be right—and you'll know you're exactly where you need to be. I encourage you to get out your gardening gloves today and get to plucking if that's what God is calling you to do!

◦⁓◦

"I know that whatever God does,
It shall be forever.
Nothing can be added to it,
And nothing taken from it.
God does it, that men should fear before
Him" (Ecclesiastes 3:14 NKJV).

Is there something you need to uproot today?

Related Readings
Luke 11:28; John 15:14; Romans 2:6

6

When You Feel As Though God Isn't Enough

*You, O L*ORD*, have not forsaken those who seek you.*

Psalm 9:10 ESV

I n *Betrayed by God? Making Sense of Your Expectations,* I wrote about a time when an ache in my heart was pushing me to the edge of obsession. I'm thankful I took my feelings to God through journaling. He used it to set me straight and remind me He alone is enough.

May 21, 2009

Every now and then, my faith is washed away in a torrential downpour of longing. In this stormy ache, everything I have learned about You, who You are, remembrance of what You have done in my life, and the truth of Your love for me is washed away in a flood of desire for satisfaction— for something or someone that promises to put an end to my longing. In these moments, when I have forgotten You, when I don't believe You are enough, I am most vulnerable to compromising what I believe, of laying You on the altar and killing my relationship with You for my own dreams, hopes, and desires I believe will satisfy.

Dreams, hopes, and desires such as love, intimacy, romance, children, sex, comfort, companionship, and significance.

When these things dominate me, and I feel that I must have them to save me, it's because I doubt that You are enough. Doubting You, doubting Your love, the doubt beckons me to trade You for an idol, a lesser love. But if I let You go, what do I have? Like the psalmist, I ask...

"Whom have I in heaven but you?" (Psalm 73:25).

Who in all of earth, all of my city, all of my home, and all of my bed at night? Whom have I but You? No one. No one compares. No, I will not kill my relationship with You by exchanging You for an idol, a lesser love, for my greatest love is You. I will not trade You in for temporary satisfaction. You last forever. Idols and lesser loves do not.

⁊

"Those who pay regard to vain idols
forsake their hope of steadfast love" (Jonah 2:8 ESV).

Have you ever believed if you could just have something or someone you desired, you would be more satisfied than you are with God? Have you believed something or someone else could save you from life, fear, loneliness, desperation, heartbreak, disappointment, or any other heart ailment?

If you are struggling with believing He is enough, talk with Him today and tell Him the truth about how you feel. Then repent and turn your heart back toward Him.

Related Readings

Psalms 16:4; 63:3; 2 Timothy 2:13

7

Love Is the Bond of Perfection

Love must be sincere.

Romans 12:9

Do you have one prayer you've repeatedly lifted up over the years? If so, I can relate. Numerous times I've begged, "Lord, please teach me how to love!" Those who know me well know I have a lot to learn about love. I'm grateful God is persistent in teaching me since I am often a slow learner.

One day, after thinking about loving God's way, He blessed me with the following thoughts, which I wrote in my journal. I hope they will encourage you to love others well.

> If beauty held within it some magic power to create lasting love, all of Hollywood would be abounding in love. If success held within it the power of committed love, all the world's richest and most powerful would be most in love. However, love does not come to dwell in perfection, for no one is perfect. Love dwells in the unlovely, the imperfect because my love for another is not produced by the object of my love. It exists *in me* when I choose to love all that is unlovely and imperfect, and I thereby receive the love I need by being the lover first.

"Love…is the bond of perfection" (Colossians 3:14 NKJV).

If I searched the world over and found that which I perceived to be perfect and therefore gave my love away, I would soon be disappointed by the illusion of perfection. I could wander my entire life on an endless search for perfect love and I would never know love.

I would never experience the joy of giving grace to another, of accepting without condition, of loving wholly with a pure heart, and not seeking for self, because love *gives*. I have fallen victim to the lies of the world if I believe I can only love the beautiful, successful, or perfect. Christ died and placed the love of His heart into mine so that I can love with His unconditional love. He loves the imperfect; He loves *me*.

"But above all these things put on love, which is the bond of perfection" (Colossians 3:14 NKJV).

How can you serve others by being the one who loves first, rather than waiting to be loved?

Related Readings
Romans 13:10; 1 Corinthians 13:4-13; 1 Peter 4:8

8

An Uncomfortable, Life-Giving Message

After desire has conceived, it gives birth to sin;
and sin, when it is full-grown, gives birth to death.

James 1:15

I used to think the consequence of sin was limited to separation from God in the form of hell or in discipline, but now I don't think so. One day it hit me that, when we choose sin, we not only go against God and His will but also choose to be our own worst enemy. We choose to wound ourselves because sin corrupts. It taints us. It makes us aware of things we never should have known. It causes us to forfeit God's best.

Through sin, we lose innocence, purity, conviction, and integrity. We lose the joy and wonder of living like a little child, unaware of evil. Tragically, we often downplay the personal consequences of sin. We think we get away with sin because we may not see any immediate consequence in our circumstances. We don't get caught. No one knows, or it's "just a little thing." But we must not downplay the effect sin has on our souls.

"The wages of sin is death" (Romans 6:23).

The woman who chooses adultery thinks, "I deserve to be happy.

My husband doesn't satisfy me." She doesn't realize that when she chooses unfaithfulness, she corrupts her own soul. She forfeits the highest virtues of selflessness, compassion, love, and obedience to God, all in the name of pleasure and self-gratification.

The woman who justifies becoming involved in a dishonest business deal corrupts her own soul as she throws away trust in God, faithfulness, and hope in the Lord's provision. When we choose sin, we never win. We always participate in our own destruction.

Maybe you have chosen sin and now you are grieving that choice. The good news is that God has said if you confess your sin, He is faithful and just to forgive your sin and to cleanse you from all unrighteousness (1 John 1:9). Daughter of God, He wants to renew your heart through His Word and in relationship with Him. I invite you to confess your sin today and invite Him to transform you. You are loved.

✑

"Whoever conceals their sins does not prosper,
but the one who confesses and renounces
them finds mercy" (Proverbs 28:13).

Do you need to confess a sin so you can receive God's cleansing forgiveness?

Related Readings
Psalm 119:133; Romans 3:23; Colossians 3:5

9

Two Choices When You Suffer Relational Heartache

The righteous...will not be afraid of evil tidings;
His heart is steadfast, trusting in the LORD.

Psalm 112:6-7 NKJV

When I met my husband, we did what a lot of couples do when they are getting acquainted—we shared stories. We shared stories about our families, about where we grew up, and about our previous relationships. Although I'd like to say all my relationships had peaceful endings, some didn't. Some included heartbreak that took a while to heal.

My guess is that you, too, have had your share of relational heartbreaks, betrayals, or disappointments. When this happens, you have two choices: you can become disillusioned and cynical, or you can become more realistic, discerning, and wise.

"Do not forsake wisdom, and she will protect you;
love her, and she will watch over you" (Proverbs 4:6).

The disillusioned cynic shuts down her heart. She stops hoping for loving relationships. But the discerning and wise woman has a better approach. She knows this world is not her home. She knows perfect relationships await only on the other side of heaven. So she accepts that people will sometimes hurt her—and she will hurt others too. She knows she has an adversary who comes to steal, kill, and destroy (John 10:10), so life will sometimes be filled with relational pain. She is realistic about the sinful condition of the world, her own heart, and the hearts of those she loves. But she is not cynical, because she knows God is at work in the most horrendous experiences—just as He was at work in the tragedy of the cross—making what is ugly into something redemptive. She knows God's love is bigger than her relational heartbreaks, so she continues to love. She lives by faith and places her trust in the Faithful One, not in man.

Oswald Chambers had it right when he wrote in *My Utmost for His Highest*, "Our Lord's confidence in God and in what His grace could do for any man, was so perfect that He despaired of no one. If our trust is placed in human beings, we shall end in despairing of everyone." Should others disappoint, hurt, or betray you, don't become cynical. Instead, be a wise woman. Love God and love people, but put your total trust in Christ.

⚜

"The Lord is my strength and my shield; my heart trusts in him, and he helps me" (Psalm 28:7).

Have you become cynical about relationships, or are you trusting in the Lord?

Related Readings
Psalms 16:8; 21:7; 55:22

How to Be Content with What You Have

*Better one handful with tranquility
than two handfuls with toil
and chasing after the wind.*

Ecclesiastes 4:6

I f you take a casual stroll around any bookstore, you'll notice the world's message that the only way to contentment is to have more and be more. You need a better body, a nicer sports car, and a better-looking spouse. You need to be more charming, more intelligent, and more influential. But this "have more, be more" message can lead to discontentment.

Hebrews 13:5 tells us, "Be content with what you have, because God has said, 'I will never leave you; never will I forsake you.'" Part of the definition of the Greek word translated "content" is "to ward off." It's related to another word meaning "to raise a barrier." This is interesting because I once thought contentment was only attained by being happy with what I have. However, these definitions remind me that being content has as much to do with keeping what's bad *out* as it does with appreciating what I already possess.

∽

"Godliness with contentment is
great gain" (1 Timothy 6:6).

I once visited a series of large, luxurious homes with a friend. My eyes drank in the beauty of the decor at each address. I admired the ornate furnishings, updated kitchens, and lush backyard landscapes. When I arrived back home, I felt empty and discontent. I was disappointed I didn't have more. Yep, just as the Bible says, we must guard against being ungrateful for what God has given—we must "raise a barrier" against anything that makes us feel discontent.

And we have to remember He blesses one with a large home while someone else with a more modest residence. He gives one person a position of leadership while another works behind the scenes. He gives to each according to His will.

We have to "raise barriers" against unrealistic "have more, be more" messages that tell us we aren't important unless we are rich, we aren't successful unless we have a high-profile job, or we aren't significant unless we are beautiful. Expectations can blind us to more important blessings we are already holding in our hands, such as love, friendships, faith—and especially eternal life. The woman who has learned to be content with what she has and knows God is the Giver of all good things is a blessed woman indeed.

∾

"The boundary lines have fallen for
me in pleasant places; surely I have a
delightful inheritance" (Psalm 16:6).

Are you content with the boundary lines God has given you? If not, how can you begin to show appreciation for His gifts today?

Related Readings
Proverbs 16:8; Luke 12:15; Philippians 4:12

The Voice of Shame

I praise you because I am fearfully and wonderfully made;
your works are wonderful, I know that full well.

Psalm 139:14

Once in a grocery store checkout line, my eyes were drawn to a magazine designed to make every woman in America feel she needs to make a better version of herself. You know the kind. The one with the supermodel on the cover looking as though she were dipped in bronze. Her white teeth, flowing hair, and perfect body make you think, "She looks like she doesn't have any problems. I bet her friends are nice and her boyfriend is amazing."

While I waited in line to pay for my apples and potato chips, I was mentally drawn to compare my body to hers. "My hips used to look like that and my hair used to be that long and beautiful." By the time I reached the cashier, there was a little voice of shame inside me saying, "You are not enough."

No one is a stranger to the voice of shame because it's the voice of the accuser (Revelation 12:10). It's the voice that reminds you that you just don't cut it. It speaks to both men and women through cultural messages, saying that to be enough, they've got to look perfect. It's the voice that says, "Your nose is too big; your lips are too small. You need this pumped up and that deflated. You need plastic surgery—and you definitely don't have a body like Ms. Cover Girl. You really should be ashamed of yourself."

ᶜ♾

"The thief comes only to steal and
kill and destroy" (John 10:10).

It wouldn't be so horrible if the goal of the voice of shame was just to make you feel bad. If that were true, every woman would see the magazine, feel a twinge of guilt, and then go on her merry way without thinking about it again. But the goal of the voice of shame is always to make you *own shame*, because when you do, shame can control you. This is always the goal of the accuser.

To move toward a biblical standard for body image, we have to move away from "It's all about me" to "It's all about God." We will care for our bodies so we can serve Him, but we will not be obsessed about them.

ᶜ♾

"Anyone who believes in him will never
be put to shame" (Romans 10:11).

Do you feel the culture has influenced you to focus more on your physical appearance than is spiritually or emotionally healthy? If so, what is one way you can bring balance to your life?

Related Readings

Genesis 1:26-27; Job 5:9; Psalm 104:24

The Power of Tears

You have kept count of my tossings;
put my tears in your bottle.
Are they not in your book?

Psalm 56:8 ESV

While I was growing up, my mom cried during touching television moments. She cried during old movies when two lovers were reconciled. She cried while watching *The Waltons* and *Little House on the Prairie*, and she even cried during Folgers Coffee commercials. Yep, stories surrounding that stuff that is good to the last drop made her weep. So I grew up in a home where tears were acceptable and normal.

Now that I am older, I value tears for a couple of reasons. First, I generally believe when we are willing to be authentically real and honest with others, they will often do the same with us. Of course, there are exceptions, but on the whole, transparency promotes transparency, so intimacy is built. When we cry with others, they may feel free to do the same.

Second, tears help us experience God more intimately. When all our posturing and posing before the Almighty is stripped away through tears, we are humbled before Him in dependency. Tears cleanse the eyes of the heart so we can see Him more clearly and experience His grace more fully.

> "Humble yourselves before the Lord,
> and he will lift you up" (James 4:10).

But not everyone is happy to shed tears either publicly or privately. For many reasons (including our histories and insecurities), shedding tears can make us feel vulnerable and out of control. That's understandable. But if you have a hard time allowing yourself to cry, you might find what the Bible says about tears enlightening and even liberating.

For example, in Luke 19:41, Jesus—the Creator, the Alpha and the Omega, the Beginning and the End—wept over Jerusalem and was grieved that the Jews did not recognize Him as Savior. The Greek word translated "wept" means more than just shedding a few silent tears—it means "to wail aloud." That's some serious crying!

Jesus wailed. David soaked his bed with tears. Joseph cried. Jacob kissed Rachel and cried aloud. Ezra threw himself on the ground and wept. In Zephaniah, shepherds wailed. In Isaiah, even brave men cried in the streets. If it's okay for Christ our Lord and other brave men to cry, isn't it okay for us to do the same in vulnerable moments?

cx/cy

> "Cast all your anxiety on him because
> he cares for you" (1 Peter 5:7).

Are you comfortable or uncomfortable with tears? What life factors have contributed to your comfort level with crying?

Related Readings
Psalms 30:5; 39:12; 139:3

13

When You're Not Compatible with the One You Love

A new command I give you: Love one another.
As I have loved you, so you must love one another.

John 13:34

There's a lot of talk out there saying two people must be compatible for a relationship to last. In his book *The Meaning of Marriage*, Timothy Keller provides a solid perspective about this topic. I hope it enlightens you whether you have already tied the knot or are single and looking for love.

> If you think of marriage largely in terms of erotic love, then compatibility means sexual chemistry and appeal. If you think of marriage largely as a way to move into the kind of social status in life you desire, then compatibility means being part of the desired social class, and perhaps common tastes and aspirations for lifestyle. The problem with these factors is that they are not durable. Physical attractiveness will wane, no matter how hard you work to delay its departure. And socio-economic status unfortunately can change almost overnight. When people think they have found compatibility based on these things, they often make the painful discovery that they have built their relationship on unstable ground. A woman "lets herself go" or a man loses his job, and the compatibility foundation falls apart.[3]

*"Love is patient, love is kind. It does not envy, it does
not boast, it is not proud" (1 Corinthians 13:4).*

When what Timothy Keller is talking about happens, a couple's sense of relational compatibility may be crushed, and they may not feel the rush of love they experienced earlier in their relationship. They won't be driven by strong feelings of love to perform mundane acts of love. They may even be deceived into thinking what they are experiencing is not love because they aren't overcome with moving emotion. If this happens, they have obviously failed to understand the truth about love: sometimes love involves moving emotions, and sometimes it does not.

Most often, love is not something you feel but something you *do*. When you *do* love, you will often *feel* love. Where your actions are, there your heart will be. This, dear friend, is a truth that can help your relationship withstand changes in compatibility.

*"Over all these virtues put on love, which binds them
all together in perfect unity" (Colossians 3:14).*

Do you need to choose to love your mate today? If you are single, do you need to take these truths to heart to be better prepared for marriage?

Related Readings
Ecclesiastes 4:9; Romans 12:10; Hebrews 13:1

14

Waiting in Ambush for God

They who wait for the Lord shall renew their strength;
they shall mount up with wings like eagles;
they shall run and not be weary;
they shall walk and not faint.

Isaiah 40:31 ESV

Are you waiting for God to reveal His plans for your life? Waiting for direction can certainly be difficult. However, remember this: without hope, waiting for God can feel like torture, but with confidence in Him, waiting can feel like joyful anticipation! Here's why.

Isaiah 30:18 says, "Blessed are all who wait for him!" The Hebrew word translated "wait" means, in part, to wait in ambush. Just thinking about this definition makes me smile. Imagine it. Waiting in ambush for God is like a happy-faced dog who knows his master is coming home, so he stays by the door, ready to pounce when he arrives. It's like a young woman who counts the minutes for her date to show up for the prom. It's like a freckle-faced boy who anticipates Christmas and counts the days until December 25.

To wait in ambush for God means hoping for the future and what He will do through us, because we know something good is going to happen—in God's time, in God's way. When faith replaces distrust, the agony of waiting can turn into hopeful anticipation.

> "I wait for the LORD, my soul waits, and in
> his word I hope" (Psalm 130:5 ESV).

To wait in ambush for God is to be fully convinced He is working behind the scenes. I allow my heart to dream about the goodness that will be mine after my wait is over. On the contrary, when I wait without dreaming, my future hopes are not hope at all, but despair. The end result of waiting in faith is always a reward. But when we wait without hope, we may act out of our unbelief through sin and run ahead of God. To wait in ambush for God means I have to choose to trust Him until He shows up. I may have to say, "Shana, what do you believe? Do you believe God is at work? Will you choose to believe He has a plan? If so, lift up your head, girl! God is on His way!"

Are you waiting for God to show you how He is going to use you for His glory? Are you in an uncomfortable in-between place? Do you need Him to answer a prayer? If so, lift up your head and wait in ambush for God. He's on His way!

❧

> "You do not lack any spiritual gift as you
> eagerly wait for our Lord Jesus Christ to
> be revealed" (1 Corinthians 1:7).

If you are in a time of waiting, are you waiting on God in joyful expectation?

Related Readings

Micah 7:7; Matthew 6:34; James 5:11

15

A Revelation About God's Love in Action

I shall delight in Your statutes;
I shall not forget Your word.

Psalm 119:16 NASB

Some things in life are too beautiful for words, like the majestic Rocky Mountains, the sound of a babbling brook, the joy of a baby's giggle—and the incredible Word of God. But for some of us, the Bible doesn't feel beautiful. Instead, it feels like a judgment against us every time we open it. When we read Scripture, all we feel is condemnation.

As I read the New Testament one day, a subtle feeling arose in me that I wasn't measuring up. Then a thought came to mind: "The conviction you are sensing is the purification of the human heart through the Word." I suddenly remembered Hebrews 4:12-13.

> For the word of God is living and active. Sharper than any doubled-edged sword, it penetrates even to dividing soul and spirit, joints and marrow; it judges the thoughts and attitudes of the heart. Nothing in all creation is hidden from God's sight. Everything is uncovered and laid bare before the eyes of him to whom we must give an account.

I thought, "Ah, yes, Lord. My soul and spirit are laid bare and exposed before You. You know everything about me. You see the thoughts and intentions of my heart, and You purify me as Your Word judges both. This is the purification of my heart through Your Word as it corrects me and shows me where I am blind."

Then an old truth hit me in a new way—the conviction I feel is God's love in action, transforming me through His Word. It's never His desire to burden us with guilt that leads to death, but to reveal our sin so we can experience life! It's to show us where our thoughts and intentions are wrong so He can lead us to what is right. Ah, joyous liberty!

The accuser wants to beat you up with how much you have failed and how much you have sinned against God. He doesn't want you to know God's grace, mercy, and love. Through God's blood, forgiveness, and love, He has made you worthy. And remember, the conviction you sense when you read the Word is God's deep love in action, working to transform you so you can experience life and a greater fullness of joy!

∽

"Your words were found, and I ate them, and your
words became to me a joy
and the delight of my heart" (Jeremiah 15:16 ESV).

Are you able to see that God's conviction is His love for you? Why or why not?

Related Readings
Psalm 119:97-98,105; Revelation 10:9

16

Have You Put God in a Blessing Box?

Surely your goodness and love will follow me
all the days of my life,
and I will dwell in the house of the LORD forever.

Psalm 23:6

Sometimes I have been guilty of trying to put God in a blessing box. I have decided where and how He will be able to bless me. Maybe you've done the same.

"Lord, I will be blessed if I live in Florida, but not in Vermont."

"Lord, I will be blessed if I use my gifts and talents at work, but not if I don't enjoy my job."

"Lord, I will be blessed if I have children, but not if I am childless."

"Lord, I will be blessed if I'm married, but not if I'm single."

The Bible is filled with stories where people tried to put God in a blessing box. Many had things happen to them they would not have chosen for themselves, things that would have made it seem as if God's blessings had been forfeited. The story of Joseph is one example. As I was reading it one day, Genesis 39:1 jumped off the page: "Now Joseph had been taken down to Egypt."

He had been *taken*. Not, "He decided he wanted to go, so he went." He had no choice. Certainly there could not have been a blessing in that box, right? Of course, we know there was because we know the end of Joseph's story. But Joseph didn't see the blessing while he was in the middle of his messy story. Genesis 40:15 reveals that Joseph didn't understand God was secretly at work to bless him and use him to be a blessing: "I was forcibly carried off from the land of the Hebrews, and even here I have done nothing to deserve being put in a dungeon."

It was only years later, after his brothers showed up and after he remembered his dreams (Genesis 42:9), that he realized God had done a great work—not in spite of but because he had been taken down to Egypt against his will. God cannot be put in a blessing box regardless of what happens to us and regardless of how the story of our lives unfold. He is always at work, and His love never fails (Psalm 136:1).

"Give thanks in all circumstances; for this is God's will for you in Christ Jesus" (1 Thessalonians 5:18).

How will knowing God cannot be put in a blessing box enable you to surrender to His plans for your life?

Related Readings
Genesis 50:19-21; Psalm 115:3; Romans 8:28

17

Set Free from Regret

*We know that in all things God works for
the good of those who love him, who have
been called according to his purpose.*

Romans 8:28

Sometimes I dance in the kitchen while I'm making dinner. But a couple of years ago, I danced a special dance I think I will always remember. I twirled. I shook. I boogied. I danced like no one was watching because no one was—except God. I danced because an overwhelming joy had filled up my heart, brought on by the realization that a regret from long ago had been eclipsed by a quiet and secure confidence.

"I am right where I belong. God really did know what He was doing." Even though there were times I didn't believe any good could come from my past, now I am sure it is as it was meant to be. Ah! Blessed internal freedom!

"But Lord, why so long? Why did it take so very long for You to bring me closure? Why did I struggle so? Why did I always question whether the choices I made set my life on a trajectory leading to the regret that haunted me? What did I receive from all those years of internal struggle?"

Then it hit me—stories. I got stories. And these stories produced life lessons for me to share with others.

> "Christ…who comforts us in all our tribulation, that
> we may be able to comfort those who are in any
> trouble, with the comfort with which we ourselves
> are comforted by God" (2 Corinthians 1:3-4 NKJV).

Joy filled my heart. "Oh! Beloved, priceless, precious stories! I know those redemptive kind can only be received through pain. Yes, Lord! These stories and life lessons are worth it! There truly was no other way. A testimony that transforms never comes easily. How could I ever comfort others if I never received comfort myself?"

Those who have received comfort, can comfort. Without pain we don't receive God's comfort in quite the same way. On this side of my dance, I would not give back the struggle. I am finally at peace with the past, so I can move into the future with clarity and without the burden of regret.

⁓

> "As a mother comforts her child, so will I
> comfort you; and you will be comforted
> over Jerusalem" (Isaiah 66:13).

Are you in a season of regret? What experience has God given you that you can now use to comfort, inspire, or guide others, not in spite of what has happened to you, but because of what has happened to you?

Related Readings
Ecclesiastes 7:10; Joel 2:24-25

18

Trusting God and Letting Go of Fear

*The holy women of the past...submitted themselves to
their own husbands, like Sarah, who obeyed Abraham
and called him her lord. You are her daughters if
you do what is right and do not give way to fear.*

1 Peter 3:5-6

When I read 1 Peter 3:5-6, I wondered, "What does fear have to do with submission?" Then I realized fear is the enemy of submission and a gentle and quiet spirit because fear can cause even the best woman (or even man) to be controlling.

Deep down the fearful woman may think, "I am afraid, so I will try to control, fix, mother, or tame my husband or even God. That way I won't get hurt. In honesty, I am terrified that if I let my husband be the leader of our home, God won't guard my back and things will get out of control, so I will try to control. This is the only way I can be safe."

So you see, fear and control are the opposite of a trusting, gentle, and quiet spirit. A controlling, fearful woman can be manipulative, condescending, passive-aggressive, or even downright rude. She's bossy because she's distrusting or prideful. Inside she is like a raging river or turbulent lake. She's bothered and without peace.

"A constant dripping on a day of steady rain and a contentious woman are alike" (Proverbs 27:15 NASB).

But the woman who trusts God like Sarah trusted Him is coura-geous. She has a gentle and quiet spirit. She is gracious in speech. She is mindful about what she says and how she says it. She knows her words and actions can build up or tear down her home (Proverbs 14:1). She's not a doormat. She's not passive. Whether outgoing, reserved, or bold, her God-given personality shines in its fullness, but it has come under the authority of the Holy Spirit (Galatians 5:22-23). She is sub-mitted to God, so she submits to the leadership of her husband (who is called to be considerate as he lives with his wife and treat her with respect—1 Peter 3:7). Her obedience brings her internal peace and rest, unlike the woman who has given way to fear and is tormented.

A wise woman knows submission is not weakness; it's wisdom. It's one way she maintains peace of mind and heart. It's how she demon-strates her trust in God.

∞

> "By wisdom a house is built, and through
> understanding it is established" (Proverbs 24:3).

Do you trust God enough to submit to your husband?

Related Readings
Proverbs 9:13-15; 21:9; 31

19

How to Experience More Joy Today

Give thanks to the Lord, for he is good;
his love endures forever.

Psalm 107:1

In my book *Betrayed by God?* I share a story about a summer day that was overcast—in the sky and in my heart. When I went for a walk near my home, the gloomy weather mirrored my mood. For some reason, I decided to find pictures in the clouds above me, just as I used to when I was little. However, when I started my game, everything I saw in the fluffy shapes looked mean. Everything had teeth. It was as if a violent zoo had filled up the heavens. A handful of beasties snarled at me from above. "Great—that's just what I need," I thought.

On my return trip home, I decided to praise God as an antidote to my cranky attitude. I thanked Him for bringing good out of what was bothering me, for being in control, for loving me—and I told Him how awesome He is.

"How magnificent are Your works,
Lord" (Psalm 92:5 HCSB).

Suddenly the clouds—both internally and externally—were transformed. And wouldn't you know it? My next glance at the sky looked different! A laughing girl with pigtails came into view, and then a happy hippo chasing a fish caught my eye. Suddenly the entire sky above me was filled with frolicking animals and at least a half-dozen giggling babies lying on their backs. Oh! Joyous praise! When it filled my mouth, the nasty external—and internal—weather was changed. I felt joy!

This brings me to an important point about prayer: When we pray about what ails us, or pour out our complaint to the Lord about what is bothering us, let's not just make requests of God—let's also give Him thanks. Why? Because thanksgiving is the "I believe" of prayer. If I pour out my anguish to God without being thankful, I experience despair; but when I thank God for what He has done and what He's going to do, I experience hope. I experience peace. This is the promise of Philippians 4:7. So when we experience nasty internal or external weather, let's not forget to follow up our petitions with a good dose of thanksgiving.

"Do not be anxious about anything, but in every situation, by prayer and petition, with thanksgiving, present your requests to God. And the peace of God, which transcends all understanding, will guard your hearts and your minds in Christ Jesus" (Philippians 4:6-7).

How can you practice gratitude today while you lift your petitions to Christ?

Related Readings
2 Chronicles 7:3; Psalms 118:24; 139; 145:9

20

Makin' It Through
Your Messy Middle

Your steadfast love, O Lord, extends to the heavens,
your faithfulness to the clouds.

Psalm 36:5 ESV

I considered going to see the film *The Chronicles of Narnia: The Lion, the Witch and the Wardrobe*. But then I learned Aslan, the great lion and main character, is killed in the movie. "Nope," I thought, "couldn't stand watching that. Would hurt my heart." I later learned Aslan comes back to life, so I decided I could handle watching since I knew the story ends well.

Keeping one's hope fixed on the promise of heaven is like watching a movie with a mess in the middle. With our gaze turned toward eternity, we can endure life's messy difficulties because we know Christ will return, we will go home to heaven, and our story will end very, very well.

⟡

"He will wipe every tear from their eyes. There will be
no more death or mourning or crying or pain, for the
old order of things has passed away" (Revelation 21:4).

Maybe like me, you have often heard about the heroes in Hebrews 11 whose faith led to great acts and rewards while alive. For instance, they shut the mouths of lions, escaped the edge of the sword, and became powerful in battle. But maybe like me, you haven't heard much about another group mentioned at the very end of the chapter. This group endured messes in the middle of their lives because they steadfastly held on to an eternal perspective (Hebrews 11:16). These folks faced jeers and flogging, were imprisoned, were sawed in two, and were put to death. They were destitute, homeless, and hungry. But they endured because they knew this world was not their home. They also knew their story would end very well.

When I consider the trials of these saints, I have to admit that my faith seems small. I am often more concerned about my comfort than I am about persevering through a trial. But sometimes keeping my eyes on eternity has helped me hold on to hope in the middle of my own messy story. It has enabled me to endure relational heartbreak, physical fatigue, financial difficulties, and the day-in, day-out challenges of life. I am happy to say that as I get closer to going home, it's becoming easier to keep my gaze turned upward.

∽

"Surely God is my salvation; I will trust and not be afraid.
The LORD, the LORD himself, is my strength and my
defense; he has become my salvation" (Isaiah 12:2).

How can you keep your gaze fixed on eternity so you have greater courage for your own "messy middle"?

Related Readings
Isaiah 25:8; 1 Corinthians 15:57; Revelation 21:4

In Search of a Pinterest-Perfect Life

Trust in the LORD and do good;
dwell in the land and enjoy safe pasture.
Take delight in the LORD,
and he will give you the desires of your heart.

Psalm 37:3-4

I like Pinterest because it's filled with lots of awesome ideas to improve just about every area of life. I can find great organizational ideas, yummy recipes, and cool art projects with just a few clicks. But if I'm not careful, Pinterest can make me believe the lie that my life can be "Pinterest perfect."

Have you noticed the desire for perfection always leads to discontent, ingratitude, a lack of peace, and even sin? But being discontent isn't our fault, right? It's Adam and Eve's fault because they weren't content with what the Lord had given them. So they took a bite of the fruit and went outside their God-given boundaries. Tragically, life has been a discontented mess for the whole human race ever since.

✍

"When the woman saw that the fruit of the tree
was good for food and pleasing to the eye, and
also desirable for gaining wisdom, she took some
and ate it. She also gave some to her husband,
who was with her, and he ate it" (Genesis 3:6).

Can you imagine how life would have turned out for us if Adam and Eve had believed what God had provided was enough? They would have been content. We're no different from Adam and Eve. Discontentment and a lack of trusting God is behind every extramarital affair, every time we lust after our friend's beautiful home, and every desire for money run amok (James 1:15). It seems we always want more than what God has given—to our destruction.

I took a trip to impoverished Africa to work with a short-term mission's organization. After I returned home, any discontent I felt about living in a small apartment was washed away with the joy of gratitude. I felt like a queen living in her castle, as my expectations adjusted and appreciation for God's provision filled my heart. If you feel discontent today, I invite you to submit to the Lord as your provider and express gratitude to Him for what He has given. Contentment will be yours when you readjust your expectations, submit to God's rule, and allow Him to sit on the throne of your life as Provider.

∽

"Be content with what you have, because
God has said, 'Never will I leave you; never
will I forsake you'" (Hebrews 13:5).

Do you struggle with believing your life has to be "Pinterest perfect"? If so, why?

Related Readings
Matthew 6:25-26; Philippians 4:12-13; Hebrews 13:5

22

Are You Praying
Cotton-Candy Prayers?

*Let us draw near with a sincere
heart in full assurance of faith.*

Hebrews 10:22 NASB

It's easy to throw God cotton-candy prayers that lack substance—in traffic, in the shower, or as we run out the door to work. It's easy to stay on the safe side of petition by asking God for things our hearts don't truly desire. Why? Because having a shallow prayer life feels safe, right?

On the contrary, praying for what we know only God can accomplish or for what we sincerely want can feel dangerous—as though our hearts have been stripped bare and made vulnerable before Him. To avoid this feeling of discomfort, what do we do? We separate our desires from prayer. We ask Him only for things that haven't captivated our affections or that we know He'll say yes to. This way we can feel like we did our duty and were faithful daughters who have stayed in communion with Christ. But is that all there is to the Christian life? Just to "pray it safe"?

      cs

"Without faith it is impossible to please Him, for he who comes to God must believe that He is and that He is a rewarder of those who seek Him" (Hebrews 11:6 NASB).

Sometimes I want to stand on the cliff edge of prayer, certain that only God can provide what I need—and that if He doesn't, disaster will be mine. There is something exhilarating about living in total desperation for Him. Other times, I want to live predictably. I don't want God to upset the apple cart of my carefully arranged life. If I insist on always being in control, I trade adventure with Him for the mundane. I forfeit an abundant Christian life for an easier life that's less threatening. Sure, I feel like I get to live in a spiritual safety zone by not asking God for too much (as if that were possible!), but I also try to put Him in a box. As a result, my heart dies.

Life with God was meant to be lived in faith. What kind of prayers have you been praying? If you're like me, you ask God for far too little. I encourage you to live on the cliff edge of prayer and ask Him to move some mountains for you while you trust Him.

⁂

> "Pray in the Spirit on all occasions with all kinds of prayers and requests. With this in mind, be alert and always keep on praying for all the Lord's people" (Ephesians 6:18).

Are you "standing on the cliff edge of prayer" or are you only praying "cotton candy" prayers?

Related Readings
Matthew 21:22; Mark 11:24; John 14:13-14

23

Maybe It's Not a Good Idea to Post That Post

Let your conversation be always full of grace, seasoned with salt, so that you may know how to answer everyone.

Colossians 4:6

I enjoy social media because it's a great way for me to keep in touch with family and friends. I like perusing the pictures they post and reading their reflections online. But sometimes social media is also grievous. Because—as perhaps you have also realized—there are few places where the condition of the human heart can be so obviously seen than online. Granted, I am often blown away by the kindness shown from one stranger to another through online platforms, but I am even more blown away by the human tendency to become quickly offended.

It seems some folks are quick to jump to conclusions, rush to judgment, and jump on the bandwagon of bad-mouthing someone they have never met because it feels safer to say mean things behind a screen than in person. But as Christians, we are called to a higher standard. It takes wisdom and care to know when and how to insert one's beliefs or opinions into an online conversation. We must remember that the most godly and loving thing to do may be to not say anything at all when online conversations get heated, and when we do speak (or text, message, tweet, or post), to be kind.

> Warn [the believers in Ephesus] before God against quarreling about words; it is of no value, and only ruins those who listen...Don't have anything to do with foolish and stupid arguments, because you know they produce quarrels. And the Lord's servant must not be quarrelsome but must be kind to everyone, able to teach, not resentful (2 Timothy 2:14,23-24).

How would the world be different if we took these words to heart? How would others see the love of Christ more clearly?

I think these words from Paul weren't just for Timothy; they are for us now as we not only speak, but text, message, tweet, and post. We are called to be a light to the world, including the online world.

✍

> "A good man brings good things out of the good
> stored up in him, and an evil man brings evil things
> out of the evil stored up in him" (Matthew 12:35).

Consider online conversations you have been a part of in the past. Have they been filled with grace and a lack of quarreling as Scripture commands? What practical steps can you take in the future to follow God's will in online communication?

Related Readings
Mark 9:50; Ephesians 4:29; 1 Peter 3:15

24

Don't Stick Your Fingers in All the Chocolates

You are my friends if you do what I command.

John 15:14

Have you ever struggled with fully obeying God? I have. Once I sensed the Lord nudging me toward obedience as though He was telling me to let go of some potential opportunities because I was giving them too much importance in my life. They were edging in on the place in my heart reserved just for Him. These opportunities were like a box of chocolates.

It was as though God was saying, "Wait! Don't eat those. I have something better for you." But because I didn't trust Him, I didn't listen. So I gave in to temptation and "stuck my fingers" in all the "chocolates of opportunity." I still wanted to check out the possibilities because I didn't trust God to show up. I wanted a backup. So I hedged the line of disobedience without completely disobeying. And because I hadn't completely submitted to Him, He wasn't ruling over me, and panic ruled my life instead.

"This is what the Sovereign LORD, the Holy One of Israel, says:
only in quietness and trust is your strength,
but you would have none of it"' (Isaiah 30:15).

Have you ever been there? Remember, we may partially obey God, but it's still disobedience. Even if we are only "partially sinning," we won't experience peace because it's only where God rules that peace reigns. We may partially obey God in a small matter like purchasing a car, or in something bigger, like getting married or following Him in a new calling. If God says to wait, or if He chooses another option for us, maybe we think, "Well, it's not really a big deal if I change things up just a little, right?" We must be careful not to deceive ourselves. We will reap what we sow (Galatians 6:7).

If an attitude of unbelief and faithlessness creeps into our hearts, the next thing we know, we may end up heading down a path we had no intention of walking. Disobedience can be a slippery slope. Be careful to guard your heart with all diligence. This is the way to peace and life!

∽

"Keep your heart with all diligence, for out of it
spring the issues of life" (Proverbs 4:23 NKJV).

Do you know what God wants you to do, and are you doing it?

Related Readings
Luke 11:28; 1 Peter 1:14; 2 John 1:6

My Life as a 9-1-1 Christian

I have told you these things, so that in me you may have peace.
In this world you will have trouble.
But take heart! I have overcome the world.

John 16:33

In some seasons of my life I have been a 9-1-1 Christian. That means I mostly prayed to God or read the Bible only in an emergency. All I needed was for my panic button to get pushed, and I was on my knees or had my face immediately in the Bible. Maybe you can relate.

When I was a teacher, I watched a scenario that reminded me of my 9-1-1 relationship with God. From an upstairs window at the school where I taught, I could see paramedics had arrived to rescue a man who had driven off the road minutes before. It struck me how different their work had been before global positioning systems became standard equipment. Paramedics had to know the city they served like the back of their hands, or they would drive around in circles and many people would die! They had to know the city by heart so they were ready to respond when they were needed.

⟳

"In all these things we are more than conquerors
through him who loved us" (Romans 8:37).

If we want to be overcomers as Scripture promises, we must tuck away God's Word in our hearts on a regular basis. Then, when we experience trouble—as we always will—we can draw on the deep well of truth He has already provided for us. If we wait until difficulty comes to reach out to Christ, we'll often panic and scramble around, trying to find peace and direction. Perhaps, like me, you can testify that this scenario is not effective!

In Matthew 4:1-11 Jesus was tempted by Satan in the wilderness. When Satan attacked Christ with lies and Jesus used Scripture from Deuteronomy for protection, He demonstrated that the only defense against deception is God's truth. Can you imagine what it would have been like had Christ not already known the truth? If He practiced 9-1-1 faith, He would have had to stop and say, "Wait a minute! I have to go look that up! I think it's somewhere in the Scriptures." Jesus sharpened His "sword of the Spirit, which is the word of God" (Ephesians 6:17) *before* the battle. He knew truth *before* He had to use it. You and I would be wise to do the same.

✑

> "I have hidden your word in my heart that I
> might not sin against you" (Psalm 119:11).

Are you hiding God's Word in your heart so you are prepared to face the trials of the day?

Related Readings
Psalm 119:103; Hebrews 4:12

26

God's Good Tests

*He knows the way that I take; when he has
tested me, I will come forth as gold.*

Job 23:10

When I was in high school, the thought of taking a test made me want to run. When I was in college, the thought of taking a test made me want to run. And when I became an adult, the thought of taking a test at the doctor's office made me want to run. No matter what kind of test, I don't like it! The good thing is God never gives a bad test. His tests are always for our good. They are also tools He uses to grow us. Here's how.

In the New International Version, Psalm 11:5 reads, "The Lord examines the righteous," while the King James Version says, "The Lord trieth the righteous." The Hebrew language helps us to understand how we got these two translations. My *Complete Word Study Old Testament* says the word translated "examine" or "trieth" is *bachan*, which means "to test, prove, examine, search out, purify, to look out, to watch. This word denotes an investigation to determine the essential qualities of an object, especially integrity."[4]

Now check this out. In its entirety, Psalm 11:5 reads like this: "The Lord examines the righteous, but the wicked, those who love violence, he hates with a passion."

When I read this Scripture and the definition of *bachan*, I got excited because the word "but" indicates that those who don't know

God *aren't tested by Him the same way those who know Him are.* There-fore, *bachan*—or testing to determine integrity and essential quali-ties—is reserved only for the righteous, and it's a privilege! Webster's describes a privilege as "a right or immunity granted as a peculiar ben-efit, advantage or favor."[5]

The word "peculiar" gives me a chuckle. Examinations and tests can certainly sometimes seem like a peculiar benefit for the person who fills the position of knowing Christ. But that is exactly how God sees them. Tests that come from Him are a privilege of position. God cares enough to test the hearts of those who know Him, which leads to greater joy because it makes us more like Him.

What you are experiencing is known by God, and it may be that He is testing your integrity, doing an investigation of your heart, and purifying you.

Are you going through a test in your finances, marriage, or faith? Aren't you glad He cares enough about you to make you more like Him?

Related Readings
Genesis 22:1; Jeremiah 20:12; James 1:12

27

When God Makes Us Wait

Those who hope in the LORD will renew their strength.
They will soar on wings like eagles; they will run and
not grow weary, they will walk and not be faint.

Isaiah 40:31

Have you been holding on to the hope of something for so long you sometimes wish your dream would die so you could be relieved of the longing? If you're like me, you've wrestled with a desire or two for years, and sometimes your heart has felt worn-out from waiting. Which brings me to some questions.

Does God intentionally take His children past the point of hoping for what they want most? Does He stand by and watch the hearts of those He loves melt in tears while their greatest desires die? Does He bring them to desperate prayer and longing?

When I look at Scripture, I have to answer yes. Sometimes He does. Sometimes God brings us to the end of ourselves, just like He did with Joseph, Hannah, Abraham, Moses, and the Israelites. But why would God, who is all-powerful and loving, not allow us to realize our desires—or make us wait so long for them to come to pass?

"Jesus told his disciples a parable to show them that they should always pray and not give up" (Luke 18:1).

I'm sure there are many reasons God does this, but one reason I find encouraging is that this is how He produces greater faith in us, granting us greater peace and joy. When we are unable to fulfill our own desires, we are forced to lean on Him rather than depend on self-sufficiency. When God backs us into the corner of unfulfilled desires, it's His chance to show there is no way except through Him. Then when He delivers the answer, He is glorified to the full. No flesh can boast in His presence. Our desperation is the stage God sets to perform His miracles so He is lifted up.

If you have been waiting for God to answer a prayer or fulfill a desire, faithfully submit yourself to Him while you wait. And be honest. Cry out like the psalmists. Tell Him your fears, frustration, and heartbreak (1 Peter 5:7). Let Him bear your burdens (Matthew 11:28). Then choose to continue to believe He has your best interests in mind while you wait for an answer. And when the answer comes, submit to His lordship.

*"Hope deferred makes the heart sick,
But when the desire comes, it is a tree
of life" (Proverbs 13:12 NKJV).*

What can you do to actively demonstrate that you are trusting God while you wait on Him?

Related Readings
Psalm 130:5-6; Proverbs 3:5-6; Lamentations 3:25

28

Fumbling Toward God's Purposes

So do not fear, for I am with you; do not be dismayed,
for I am your God. I will strengthen you and help you;
I will uphold you with my righteous right hand.

Isaiah 41:10

I have known a few women who wanted guarantees. They wanted guarantees that if they moved, took a new job, started a new career, or had a child, everything would go smoothly without feelings of failure. But because there are no such guarantees in life, they never got started toward God's plan for them.

In his book *Better Than Good*, Zig Ziglar tells the story of attending his three-year-old granddaughter's dance recital. Zig watched as a group of little pixies fumbled through their performance without a clue they were messing up. They were too busy having a great time and had never been introduced to the word "failure." I love that, don't you? Kids don't know failure is a part of life until someone tells them so. Until then, they sing, but poorly; they dance, but without rhythm; and they tell jokes that aren't funny. But when you smile and say, "You're amazing!" they look at you and say, "I know."

Sadly, on the journey from being a kid to an adult, we forget foibles while we're dancing toward God's dreams for our lives are okay, and that failure always precedes success. After all, all human beings fall before they can walk and jabber before they can talk. Why do we think we shouldn't experience failure as we age?

"You need to persevere so that when you
have done the will of God, you will receive
what he has promised" (Hebrews 10:36).

If we don't make mistakes, we have ceased to learn. And if we insist on perfection, we may never start on the journey toward a God-given purpose. Sometimes our fears are so great that we never start a project without absolute certainty of success. Fear of failure will always destroy motivation and productivity.

Granted, God doesn't give us guarantees, but He does give us Himself, because He's interested in developing our faith. We can always count on His presence (Hebrews 13:5). Will you dare to be like Zig's granddaughter and dance toward God's purposes—even if you feel as though you'll fumble all the way to heaven? If you practice long enough, God will teach you, and you'll be better than you ever imagined!

Will you dare to trust God with the unknown?

Related Readings
Exodus 14:13; Isaiah 40:29; Romans 8:31

29

How Courage and Rejoicing Are Contagious

Though he slay me, yet will I hope in him.

Job 13:15

When my husband and I visited a park in our town, at first I didn't notice anything special about the trees next to the walking path. But then I saw that each one had a plaque at its base with the name of a former president of the city council and his or her dates of service engraved on it. As we read each plaque, we talked about how the trees are a celebration and visual reminder of each president's legacy.

Everyone leaves behind a legacy, and our legacies can be good or bad.

My dear friend Maxine passed away in 2012 from cancer, but before she went running off to heaven with Jesus, she left behind a good legacy of how to rejoice. Max faced cancer with stubborn hopefulness and fervent trust in Christ. Her final days were spent praising Him and living in awe of His goodness. Just days before her death, tears filled her eyes as she said, "Shana, you would not believe the blessings that have come to me during this time." Maxine left a legacy to those around her of how to rejoice in suffering. She demonstrated what it looks like to live out Romans 5:2-4.

> We rejoice in the hope of the glory of God. Not only that,
> but we rejoice in our sufferings, because we know that

suffering produces endurance, and endurance produces
character, and character produces hope (ESV).

Once when I read this Scripture, I thought, "Rejoicing when we see
God's glory in our lives is easy. Rejoicing when we are hoping for God's
glory to be revealed is a little more difficult. And rejoicing when we
are suffering can be just plain hard." However, when we rejoice in our
sufferings—not in spite of, but because of our sufferings—the world
takes note because it's so unlike the world. And just like Maxine, we
leave behind a legacy of how to rejoice.

So you see, rejoicing during trouble isn't just for our benefit. It's
for the benefit of others, too, because it gives them courage to press
through their own trials. Like Billy Graham once said, "Courage is
contagious. When a brave man takes a stand, the spines of others are
often stiffened."

Could it be that one of the greatest legacies you can leave behind is
not showing others how to manage finances well, build businesses,
or be an excellent teacher, but how to rejoice in suffering?

Related Readings
Psalm 25:5; Isaiah 12:2; Habakkuk 3:17-18

30

How to Experience Peace While You Work

You will keep in perfect peace
those whose minds are steadfast,
because they trust in you.

Isaiah 26:3

Some women balance the demands of work or a calling with extraordinary grace. They calmly endure crises with joy, they patiently wait for God to act when things go awry, and they confidently navigate numerous daily pressures. Then some of us panic, burn ourselves out striving while we work, and worry ourselves into fitful nights without sleep.

In many seasons I have experienced peace while working hard. But in others work demands and seemingly impossible tasks threatened to steal all joy. So I have asked myself, "How do I work without striving so I can still experience internal rest and peace while I work? How do I push forward through the day and face its demands without becoming a victim of panic or worry?"

"I have told you these things, so that in me you may
have peace. In this world you will have trouble. But
take heart! I have overcome the world" (John 16:33).

In his study on Hebrews, John MacArthur writes this:

> Rest does not mean free from all nuisances and hassles; it means freedom from being so easily bothered by them. Rest means to be inwardly quiet, composed, peaceful. To enter God's rest means to be at peace with God (Romans 5:1) to possess the perfect peace He gives (Isaiah 26:3)... Rest involves remaining confident, keeping trust. In other words, to rest in something or someone means to maintain our confidence in it or him.[6]

Internal rest is found in belief and trust in God—even while we work. Belief that God's promises are true, that He is who He says He is, and trust that we are enveloped in His power and lavish love to accomplish all that concerns us. Remember, the one who hears God's promises but does not believe them is not the one who experiences internal rest. People who do not believe and trust cannot rest while they work even if they want to. Because of their unbelief, they are always driven to striving, worry, panic, or restlessness. Do you want to experience internal rest and peace while you work? Choose to trust God today and tell Him you know He has all things that concern your life and work under His control. Let Him carry your burdens.

ꝏ

> "We remember before our God and Father your
> work produced by faith, your labor prompted
> by love, and your endurance inspired by hope in
> our Lord Jesus Christ" (1 Thessalonians 1:3).

Do you have fears you need to take to God so you can experience the peace He promises?

Related Readings
John 14:27; Philippians 4:6-7; 2 Thessalonians 3:16

31

Redefining True Success

For we are co-workers in God's service.
1 Corinthians 3:9

I once volunteered at She Speaks in North Carolina where over 800 women showed up with their luggage and fragile dreams. The conference, produced by Proverbs 31 Ministries, is designed to help writers and speakers maximize their gifts of communication to glorify God. On the first day of the event, I had the opportunity to speak with many delightful ladies, but one short conversation stands out. "God has given me a book idea. I have a book proposal and I am meeting with a publisher this weekend." She grinned, but concern darkened her eyes. "I know there is a big chance for failure." I wanted to offer a word of encouragement, so I said, "That depends on how you define success. If you define it as obedience to God, you will never fail."

Over the weekend, I mulled over the idea of defining success as obedience, and I considered how our society praises those who get noticed and are at the top of their game. Even in Christianity, we worship Christian superstars. To the world, this is success. But God defines true success as obedience demonstrated by a heart that desires to please Him. That's it. That's all. Nothing more. Nothing less. When I think about success defined God's way, I have to admit a fleshy, carnal part of me wants to scream, "No, God! I want to be in charge of my own life! I want controlled outcomes!" (Isn't there a bit of control freak in all of us?) Accepting that true success is defined as obedience means I have to let go of control and let God lead while trusting Him with the results. Romans 8:14 says, "For as many are led by the Spirit of God, these are the sons of God" (NKJV). And Luke 9:23 says, "If anyone would come after me, let him deny himself and take up his cross daily and follow me" (ESV).

God isn't looking for insecure people promoting themselves and pushing their own agendas. He is looking for those who are sold out for Him and are willing to be led by Him.

Regardless of what we want to accomplish, we must remember that when the need to succeed is fueled by self-promotion, rather than by the desire to please Christ, the result will be a barren soul. Only following Jesus leads to the abundant life He promises.

⁂

"Whoever has my commands and keeps them
is the one who loves me" (John 14:21).

Do you define success as obedience? Why or why not?

Related Readings
2 Chronicles 16:9; Mark 12:41-44

32

A Message We All Need to Hear About Following Christ

Anyone who loves their life will lose it, while anyone who hates their life in this world will keep it for eternal life.

John 12:25

The older I get and the longer I walk with Christ, the more I realize Jesus said some really hard-to-swallow things. Things that have made me realize Christ wants to be our greatest affection. He doesn't just want to be a priority; He wants preeminence in our lives.

In Luke 14:26-27, Jesus says, "If anyone comes to me and does not hate father and mother, wife and children, brothers and sisters—yes, even their own life—such a person cannot be my disciple. And whoever does not carry their cross and follow me cannot be my disciple."

Jesus isn't saying we should literally hate people, but that there shouldn't be anyone, or anything, more important to us than Him, not even our own lives. We are called to follow Him no matter the cost. If He calls us to stay in a difficult marriage, we stay and follow the Master. If He calls us to move to a new state, we go and follow the Master. If He calls us to lay down our dream to move back to a place we lived before, we do that too. We follow the Master. We must love Jesus more than our very lives. Otherwise, we can't be His disciple. Not necessarily because He forbids it, but because it's *impossible*. Why? *Because a disciple follows. That's what they do.* Just like a fish swims or a bird flies.

Inevitably Christ will call the disciple to do what is contrary to their greatest affections, so they must love Him most.

I know this isn't one of those "Yay! God is going to bless you big time" messages most of us like to hear. But it's a message we *need* to hear—and hear with our hearts lest we fool ourselves into thinking we are serving Christ when we are only serving ourselves.

∾

"Then Jesus said to His disciples, 'If anyone wishes
to come after Me, he must deny himself, and take
up his cross and follow Me'" (Matthew 16:24 NASB).

Is anything standing between you and your Lord? Do you need to give up anything so you can go where He is calling? Will you let Him have His way?

Related Readings
Psalm 73:25-26; Revelation 12:11

33

Do You Believe in the Bigness of God's Love?

But the steadfast love of the LORD is from everlasting to everlasting on those who fear him.

Psalm 103:17 ESV

I once attended a Bible study where the leader asked the group, "What are some completely insensitive things people say when you are hurting?" One young woman raised her hand. "When you tell someone your problems and they say, 'God loves you.' That really irritates me."

Others chimed in and said that, yes, saying "God loves you" when someone is hurting is completely insensitive. I understand that "God loves you" can translate into "The horrible emotions you feel right now are not valid." Women—and men—certainly want others to listen and give a sensitive ear to our troubles. We don't want them to slap a pat, trite, Christian answer on our problem in an attempt to fix us. But here are a few things to think about: Does the phrase "God loves you" ever seem trite because we are unbelieving? Does it ever seem unhelpful because we are selfish? Does it ever feel meaningless because our hearts are hardened to the magnificent bigness of the love of God?

"I pray that you may have the power to comprehend, with all the saints, what is the breadth and length

and height and depth, and to know the love of Christ
that surpasses knowledge, so that you may be filled
with all the fullness of God" (Ephesians 3:17-19).

In his book *The Problem of Pain*, C. S. Lewis wrote, "The problem of reconciling human suffering with the existence of God who loves, is only insoluble so long as we attach a trivial meaning to the word 'love' and look on things as if man were the center of them."[7] When we think God's love is a little thing compared to our big problems, we have forgotten that God's love is a big thing compared to our little problems. No matter how big our problem, bigger is the love of God. No matter how deep our problem, deeper is the love of God. No matter how painful or difficult or tragic, greater still is the love of God.

Oh! If we could get this truth, how would the troubles of life shrink in comparison? Not that we wouldn't hurt, not that tears wouldn't flow, but we would know that an all-powerful, all-loving God has our back.

⁓

"God so loved the world, that he gave his only
Son, that whoever believes in him should not
perish but have eternal life" (John 3:16 ESV).

Has the phrase "God loves you" ever felt trite to you because of your unbelief?

Related Readings
Psalm 103:11-12; John 15:13; Galatians 2:20

34

Overcoming the Fear of What Other People Think

*When I am afraid, I will trust in you. In God,
whose word I praise, in God I trust; I will not be
afraid. What can mortal man do to me?*

Psalm 56:3-4

Have you ever feared doing something you know you should do because you feared criticism? If so, be encouraged. Throughout Scripture, women and men who were called to act for God experienced criticism. When Moses led the children of Israel through the desert, he cried out to God because those who followed him blamed and criticized him (Exodus 17:4). Paul was labeled as overzealous, unimpressive in person, and insincere (2 Corinthians 10:10). And nine of Jesus's remaining disciples were martyred for their faith—surely they were criticized.

God wants to give you the courage to say no to the fear of criticism and yes to Him. Isaiah 53:4 (NKJV) is a reminder that Jesus was despised, rejected, and not esteemed. He is well acquainted with the battle we face with criticism. He understands.

*"Surely He has borne our griefs and
carried our sorrows; yet we esteemed Him
stricken, smitten by God and afflicted."*

Can you imagine what Jesus's life would have been like if He had feared criticism and been self-protective? After being mocked by political groups, old and young men, and spiteful Pharisees, He would have thought twice about who He would associate with and what He would say in His final hours on earth. Rather than keeping His mouth shut when He was falsely accused, He would have defended Himself. When His enemies spit in His face, He would have retaliated. When they called Him names, He would have called down a legion of angels. When they marched Him to Golgotha, He would have run. And rather than laying down His life to give His all to those He loved, He would have held on to it—and the redemption of the human race would have been lost in His misguided passion of self-protection and the fear of criticism.

Don't allow the fear of criticism to keep you from being a gift to others. The Lord wants to help others through you. If you struggle with the fear of criticism and what others think, ask God to give you the courage to move forward in the face of criticism. His grace will give you courage.

c✧⁄ₒ

"Fear of man will prove to be a snare, but whoever trusts in the LORD is kept safe." (Proverbs 29:25)

Do you believe that the same power that enabled Jesus to say no to fearing men and yes to pleasing God is available to you?

Related Readings
2 Timothy 1:7; 1 John 4:18; Psalm 27:1

35

God Sees Your Grief

Commit your way to the LORD; trust in him, and he will act.

Psalm 37:5

Have you ever wondered why God sometimes seems inconsistent in compassion and love? Why He answers the prayer of a little girl for a puppy but denies the request of a woman to be healed from cancer? Why He allows school shootings, AIDS, and terrorist attacks, but gives a woman a new job when she asks?

If we consider the woes of humanity long enough and believe the lies that God is involved here (but not there), in this issue (but not in that one), we can start to sound like Asaph in Psalm 10:1, who asked, "O LORD, why do you stand far off? Why do you hide yourself in times of trouble?"

We may believe the lie that God is passive about heavy issues like world hunger, sex trafficking, and Internet pornography, so He is certainly not involved with smaller problems, such as the grief caused by these tragedies, right? Thankfully, the psalmist Asaph has an answer for us. Even though he wondered where God was in Psalm 10:1, by the time he came to verse 14, he embraced the truth when he wrote, "But you, God, see the trouble of the afflicted; you consider their grief and take it in hand."

The word "grief" in this passage is the word *ka'as* in Hebrew. The amazing part of this word is that the most nominal forms of it involve the trouble man causes, triggering hurt feelings. From my experience,

I know hurt feelings don't have to involve deep pain. Rather, they can involve just a small twinge of grief. Isn't it comforting that, according to this definition of grief, God notices all your grief, even when it seems small or insignificant?

"He does not willingly bring affliction or grief to anyone" (Lamentations 3:33).

When was the last time you felt grief? Was it when your spouse spoke a sharp word to you? When you lost your job? When your children let you down? No matter how insignificant your grief seems, God notices. Not only that, but He has also considered it to take it in hand.

Related Readings
Psalms 6:25; 22:8; 55:22

36

God's Good Enough

To the praise of the glory of His grace, by which
He made us accepted in the Beloved.

Ephesians 1:6 NKJV

I know a woman whose belief about what it means to be good enough for God is tangled up with messages from her father. She says she believes God loves her, but her behavior reveals otherwise. She wrestles with perfectionism and has a difficult time accepting God's grace for her sin. What she believes about being acceptable to God is tangled up with messages from her dad because, to her dad, nothing she did while she was growing up was quite good enough.

Her theology about what it means to be good enough for God is based on lies. Thankfully, for everyone who believes they have to earn favor with God, Christ has given us what we need to untangle the mess of being a performance-driven Christian. He has given us His good enough. He has given us His righteousness.

❧

"I delight greatly in the LORD; my soul rejoices
in my God. For he has clothed me with
garments of salvation and arrayed me in a
robe of his righteousness" (Isaiah 61:10).

"Righteousness" is one of those words that can be hard to understand, but in a broad sense it means "being made acceptable [good enough] to God." And through Christ's gift of salvation on the cross, He has given us righteousness that comes by faith (Romans 10:6). But receiving this gift of God's good enough, and to be freed from the pressure of being a performance-driven Christian, we must realize that in ourselves we aren't good enough for Him. We can do nothing to earn His favor—and that is liberating!

When we realize we can't create our own righteousness, then we can receive God's grace with humility. But this means we have to lay aside pride, fear, human reason, and the traditions of mankind. For people who feel they must perform for God because they believe He is a mean or hard taskmaster, life is a constant burden. Daily failures and sin are a source of shame (Romans 10:11). But, oh! What incredible freedom there is in receiving God's gift of good enough. We can stop striving and wrestling and trying to make Him love us by doing more (Romans 10:5-7).

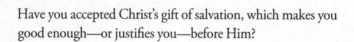

"It is with your heart that you believe and are justified, and it is with your mouth that you profess your faith and are saved" (Romans 10:10).

Have you accepted Christ's gift of salvation, which makes you good enough—or justifies you—before Him?

Related Readings
Romans 8:30; 10:9

37

How to Experience Greater Fulfillment

For you, brethren, have been called to liberty;
only do not use liberty as an opportunity for the
flesh, but through love serve one another.

Galatians 5:13 NKJV

In our society, we're told we've got to dream big, make big money, and run a big organization to be successful. Certainly, all those things are grand if they are God's assignment for you. But when they're not—and even if they are—we should never forsake big, little acts of love that are valuable and priceless to Christ. These little gestures prove our love for God—and others—is real. And they are not insignificant. These little sacrifices, when accumulated, come back to us, filling our hearts with joy and shaping our characters into something noble.

When I consider the moments when I have experienced the most fulfillment springing from love and joy, they haven't been when I have stood before a crowd to give a presentation. They haven't been when I have received a promotion or a new book deal. They have been when God allowed me to serve a sick friend, mentor a little girl, or visit a nursing home. Through these big, little acts of love, I have learned excitement often comes from accomplishments, but feelings of deep joy are a by-product of serving others with God's love.

> "These things I have spoken to you, that My joy
> may remain in you, and that your joy may be
> full. This is My commandment, that you love one
> another as I have loved you" (John 15:11-12 NKJV).

Expressing God's love in little ways has become more important to me because I failed so miserably at it in the past. Because I wanted to accomplish something great for God, I often dismissed the smaller opportunities to express His love to others. Because I was so busy, I didn't have time to listen to someone's story. Because my daily to-do list left me without margin, I didn't have time to put even a birthday card in the mail. I became self-focused.

Now I know I am more fulfilled focusing on serving those around me than I was when I was only interested in doing something big for God. If you want to experience greater joy, determine to implement little acts of love that sometimes seem insignificant.

෴

> "Whoever wants to become great among you
> must be your servant, and whoever wants to be
> first must be a slave of all" (Mark 10:43-44).

Do you find it easy or difficult to serve others in small ways?

Related Readings
1 Corinthians 9:19; Philippians 2:5-7; 1 John 2:6

38

How to Handle Rejection

*Strive for peace with everyone, and for the
holiness without which no one will see the Lord.*

Hebrews 12:14 ESV

Have you noticed sometimes God will allow us to be exposed to the very thing that frightens us so we will realize we are not victims, but instead can be victors? This is how it was for me with rejection. Twenty-five years ago possible rejection was the relational difficulty that terrified me, whether with a romantic interest or friend, so I tried to avoid it at all costs by people pleasing—which of course, didn't work.

Much to my horror, God didn't shield me from rejection like I hoped. Instead, it seemed like someone was tossing me aside every time I turned a corner. It wasn't fun! One day I woke up and realized what I thought would destroy me, hadn't! The result was what I believe God had in mind: freedom from the fear of rejection. One admonition that helped me realize rejection wouldn't destroy me is Romans 12:18, which says, "If it is possible, as far as it depends on you, live at peace with everyone."

In my twenties, I faced a particularly difficult heartbreak. I hurt someone close to me, and no matter how many times I asked for forgiveness, no matter how many tears I cried, no matter how many times I said I was sorry, it wasn't enough. The friend I hurt didn't want to have anything to do with me anymore. I struggled with so much incessant guilt and blame until God showed me Romans 12:18. It was then that

I realized I had done all I could and I was able to accept Christ's forgiveness even if my friend didn't grant forgiveness.

Certainly God calls us to do everything possible to live at peace with others. But sometimes, even though you have done "as far as it depends on you" (you have prayed, humbled yourself, forgiven, and followed the scriptural guidelines for peacemaking), the other person may not want to reconcile. Instead, he or she rejects you. When this happens, you can walk away from the relationship knowing you did all you could in obeying God because you followed Romans 12:18.

"Let us pursue the things which make for
peace and the things by which one may
edify another" (Romans 14:19 NKJV).

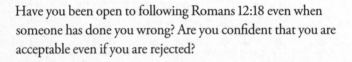

Have you been open to following Romans 12:18 even when someone has done you wrong? Are you confident that you are acceptable even if you are rejected?

Related Readings
Psalm 34:14; Matthew 5:5; Galatians 5:22-23

39

Is God Calling You to Plant a New Field?

He gives power to the weak, and to those
who have no might He increases strength.

Isaiah 40:29 NKJV

Imagine a farmer is growing beans. The beans are growing well in the same field where the farmer has planted them for the last few years. One day God calls him to plant a new crop in a new field, but there's a problem. Growing the beans is already taking all the farmer's financial and physical resources, and he doesn't feel confident about taking the risk to make a change.

If he wants to grow the new crop God has assigned, the farmer will have to resist fear. But imagine that instead the farmer says, "I can't plant and grow a new crop because it's going to be too hard. I don't have the money; I'll have to buy another piece of land. There's too much risk involved."

When God says, "Stop what you are doing. I want you to leave that field and come plant in this one over here," and we allow fear to dictate our response, we may refuse to leave our "field of security" to plant in God's new field. But God promises He will enable us to accomplish what He has called us to do.

"I can do all things through Christ who
strengthens me" (Philippians 4:13 NKJV).

Fear will make us want to cease what we are doing—or never begin
something new. So we must keep our eyes firmly fixed on the One who
is able to empower us to accomplish the task. Remember, what you
focus on will either fuel fear or fuel enthusiasm.

Be encouraged. When God calls you from an old "field" to a new
one, you can move forward in confidence because you belong to Him.
For this reason, you do not have the spirit of fear that would cause you
to live a self-directed life rather than obey God's calling. God will provide for you as you step out and make the adjustments necessary to follow Him into the unknown.

"God has not given us a spirit of fear, but of power and
of love and of a sound mind" (2 Timothy 1:7 NKJV).

Is God calling you to plant in a new field? If so, is anything
holding you back from obeying His call?

Related Readings
Isaiah 41:10; John 15:4-5; Colossians 1:11

40

No More Striving to Be a Good Christian

"Not by might nor by power, but by my Spirit," says the LORD Almighty.

Zechariah 4:6

I belong to a fantastic group that meets each Tuesday morning. The women in our little gathering share their lives, prayers, and thoughts about our weekly Bible study. Our current teacher is excellent and the content is biblically based, but I have to admit that I recently felt disheartened by a list in the back of our workbook. This list, which outlines the characteristics of those who are living an abundant life in Christ, made my chest tighten.

Among other things, the woman who is living an abundant life in Christ casts anxiety and care on God (1 Peter 5:7); hears the voice of God (John 10:27); displays the fruit of God's Spirit in daily living (5:22-23); and is content with what she has (Philippians 4:12; Hebrews 13:5). Don't get me wrong, all of these things are true, and there is nothing wrong with this list. But I couldn't help but feel discouraged because it felt like a "how to be a good Christian" checklist. "I must be this," "I must do that," "I have to work myself up to be a better woman." And that made me tired, because even on my best day, I do all these things imperfectly.

> "As it is written: 'There is no one righteous,
> not even one'" (Romans 3:10).

When I looked at this list through the lens of performance, I got discouraged. But Christianity is not supposed to be a self-improvement program. It's supposed to be about a love affair with the Savior, and out of that relationship flow good works. When I first read this list with the mind-set of "doing better," I felt internally exhausted. But then my frustration turned to joy when I remembered I am totally inadequate to accomplish one single thing on that list on my own. My ability comes through Christ and my relationship with Him. No more pulling myself up by the bootstraps. No more attempt at self-sufficiency. No more striving.

If you belong to Christ, you don't have to be performance-driven. You just have to own your sinfulness and desperation so you can receive His empowerment to be all He has called you to be.

∞

> "By their own sword they did not possess the
> land, and their own arm did not save them, but
> Your right hand and Your arm and the light of Your
> presence, for You favored them" (Psalm 44:3 NASB).

Do you believe God wants to empower you to live the Christian life? Why or why not?

Related Readings
Psalms 20:6; 42:11; 2 Corinthians 4:7

41

Intimacy with the Almighty

*I am the good shepherd. I know my
own and my own know me.*

John 10:14 ESV

The time I get quiet with the Lord is my favorite part of the day. It's when He most often reveals His truth to me, guides me, convicts me of sin, and gives me the joy of knowing I am deeply known. But I have to admit in some seasons it wasn't easy to spend time reading my Bible and praying. So many things were pulling on me that I didn't make time for what was most important in my life: intimacy with the Almighty. And then other times I was convinced it wasn't all that important to get alone with God. I bought into the lie that reading His Word wasn't all that necessary for life. Sure, I believed the Bible was true, but I could deal with life mostly on my own, right?

To experience the freedom and guidance Christ promises, that flows out of knowing Him intimately, we need to spend time with Him regularly through Bible reading and prayer. It's not a matter of legalism; it's a matter of internal life and death. It's a matter of being a disciple of Christ.

*"My sheep hear My voice, and I know them,
and they follow Me" (John 10:27 NKJV).*

During the solitude and silence of our reading His Word and praying, God gives us what we need each day. He guides and gives us His life-giving perspective. He gives us light for our paths (Psalm 119:105). In silence, we also become aware of attitudes, thoughts, and movements of the soul that go unnoticed during the busyness of the day. Silence is to the believer what weeding is to the gardener. Silence enables us to hear from God more clearly so we can, with the aid of the Holy Spirit and the Word, uproot ungodly attitudes and emotions that choke God's will out of our lives. The *Life with God Bible* says, "Solitude is the creation of an open, empty space in our lives by purposely abstaining from interaction with other human beings, so that, freed from competing loyalties, we can be found by God."[8] What can be better than knowing we are known, experiencing guidance, healing, hope, and joy through intimate time with the Savior?

"The word of God is alive and active. Sharper than any double-edged sword, it penetrates even to dividing soul and spirit, joints and marrow; it judges the thoughts and attitudes of the heart" (Hebrews 4:12).

If you aren't spending regular time with Him, what's keeping you from doing so?

Related Readings
Jeremiah 23:29; 2 Corinthians 10:4-5

42

What Does It Mean to Be One?

I and the Father are one.

John 10:30

One evening over dinner with a friend, we spoke about intimacy and what it means to be truly intimate. She shared a cute little phrase with me to remind me of intimacy's real meaning. "It means 'in-to-me-see,'" she said. Ah, yes. It's a blending of our heart with another's, so we can "see into" who they really are, and they can "see into" us.

According to Dictionary.com, intimacy is defined as, "showing a close union or combination of particles or elements: *an intimate mixture*." Being intimate involves the mixing of our life with another's, a mingling of souls, a sharing of hearts. We all long for intimacy because God designed us to connect.

> "I do not ask on behalf of these alone, but for those also who believe in Me through their word, that they may all be one; even as You, Father, are in Me and I in You, that they also may be in Us, so that the world may believe that You sent Me" (John 17:20-21 NASB).

Maybe you are wondering about sex. Granted, sex is a part of intimate expression, but it is not intimacy. In his book *Soul Cravings*, Erwin Raphael McManus writes:

"Sex can be the most intimate and beautiful expression of love, but we are only lying to ourselves when we act as if sex is proof of love. Too many men demand sex as proof of love; too many women have given sex in hopes of love. We live in a world of users where we abuse each other to dull the pain of aloneness. We all long for intimacy, and physical contact can appear as intimacy, at least for a moment."[9]

Real intimacy is not found just by merging bodies in sex. I can't help but think that, when Jesus said, "And the two shall become one" (Matthew 19:5), He meant more than just the physical. After all, how many couples share their bodies, but not their hearts? Undoubtedly, many of these people would say they are lonely. Why? Because just as a garden hose is not the source of water, but only an expression or vehicle for it, so sex is not the source of intimacy, but an outlet or expression of it.

⁓

"Let marriage be held in honor among all, and let the marriage bed be undefiled, for God will judge the sexually immoral and adulterous" (Hebrews 13:4 ESV).

Have you ever tried to achieve intimacy through sex and been disappointed?

Related Readings
Genesis 2:24; John 13:35; 15:13; 1 Corinthians 7:2

43

When God Doesn't
Say Yes to Your Prayer

*The LORD is good to all; he has
compassion on all he has made.*

Psalm 145:9

once spoke at a conference where a woman told me her husband was experiencing an extended season of unemployment. This had been very hard on their family both financially and emotionally. "We have prayed and prayed, and still nothing. We have claimed a new job over and over in Jesus's name but my husband still can't find a job."

My heart went out to her. No doubt this was tough. But as we spoke, I was reminded that we can't manipulate God through prayer because prayer is not about a formula. Naming something and claiming it doesn't guarantee a favorable answer. Prayer is not like a candy machine where I deposit the right kind of prayer and God gives me the answer I want. Prayer is about a relationship.

❧

"Pray in the Spirit on all occasions with all kinds
of prayers and requests" (Ephesians 6:18).

Don't get me wrong—prayer can change anything, and the Bible says to bring all kinds of prayers to Him. But God knows the difference between being used and bossed around and a humble petition. If you aren't sure what your motive is, ask God to show you. Also remember this: any doctrine that promises a pain-free life if only we believe enough, do enough good works, or pray hard enough is setting us up for a nasty fall, right into a pit of believing God can't be trusted. Jesus clearly states, "[He] sends rain on the righteous and the unrighteous" (Matthew 5:45) and "In this world you will have trouble. But take heart! I have overcome the world" (John 16:33). To deny that trouble touches everyone is to deny the existence of sin.

If you are struggling with trusting God because He isn't answering your prayers the way you desire, it's understandable that you would be hurting. But rather than believe He is not good or that He doesn't love you, choose to trust Him. Choose to trust His sovereignty and timing. You'll be glad you did.

∽

"Give thanks to the LORD, for he is good; his
love endures forever" (Psalm 107:1).

Have you ever struggled with believing God was good or that He loves you because life didn't turn out the way you wanted?

Related Readings
Psalms 36:5; 100:5; 119:68

44

God's Guidance Isn't Like a GPS

*I will lead the blind by ways they have not known,
along unfamiliar paths I will guide them; I will
turn the darkness into light before them and
make the rough places smooth. These are the
things I will do; I will not forsake them.*

Isaiah 42:16

Perhaps like you, sometimes I have wanted God to give me the big picture of my future so I could have peace and know I wasn't totally making a mess of His plans. But perhaps also like you, I have come to learn God never reveals the entirety of the future to His children.

In his book *The Fulfillment Factor*, Mike Kendrick writes, "Having a vision for your future isn't like having a GPS in your car. You can and should make long-term plans, but God will never give you every detail about your future. You won't be able to see the entire 'map' of your vision up front. Only a few of the main intersections will be marked."[10] The Bible echoes Mike's sentiments. Scripture says God's Word is a light for your path (Psalm 119:105). It doesn't shine like you're in broad daylight, casting clarity on every step from where you are to where you'll be next year. Instead, the Lord—and His Word—will give you just enough light for the step you're on.

✏

"Whether you turn to the right or to the left,

your ears will hear a voice behind you, saying,
'This is the way; walk in it'" (Isaiah 30:21).

If we insist that God reveal every step between where we are and the fulfillment of a revealed promise, we rob ourselves of the *abundant joy* that comes from *walking* with Him, of moving when He moves, of responding to His direction on a moment-by-moment basis, and of seeing Him orchestrate the events of our lives in surprising ways. This is what it means to keep in step with the Spirit.

"Since we live by the Spirit, let us keep in
step with the Spirit" (Galatians 5:25).

How does it make you feel to know life can be an adventure in trust as you allow God to slowly reveal the path before you?

Related Readings
Psalms 3:5-6; 25:8-9; 32:8; Jeremiah 6:16

45

What I Used to Believe About Love

Follow the way of love.

1 Corinthians 14:1

As a young woman I believed I could recognize true love because it would be consistently characterized by exhilarating emotions. It's no surprise I thought love could be defined mainly as emotion because I grew up feeding on happily-ever-afters through pop music, television, and Disney movies. I now know something very different: if we reduce love to emotion, it makes for very unsteady relationships. Emotions, like the waves of the ocean, roll in and roll out. One moment they are here, the next day they are gone. A wise woman doesn't allow her fickle emotions to choose the temperature of her relationships. Instead, she *chooses love by doing love.* And while she is doing love out of commitment, she does not fear. She knows as sure as the ocean tide rolls in and out, her pleasant feelings of love will return.

In his book *The Meaning of Marriage*, Timothy Keller writes:

> In any relationship, there will be…spells in which your feelings of love dry up. And when that happens you must remember that the essence of marriage is that it is a covenant, a commitment, a promise of future love. So what do you do? You do the acts of love, despite your lack of feeling. You may not feel tender, sympathetic, and eager to please, but in your actions you must BE tender, understanding, forgiving and helpful. And, if you do that, as time goes on

you will not only get through the dry spells, but they will become less frequent and deep, and you will become more constant in your feelings. This is what can happen if you decide to love.[11]

❧

> "A new command I give you: Love one
> another. As I have loved you, so you must
> love one another" (John 13:34).

This truth of doing love applies not just to marriage, but to every relationship in which God calls us to love when we don't feel love. Don't be deceived by reducing love to feelings. If you do, your relationships will be tossed by the winds of circumstance. But if you make love a choice as God has commanded us to do, you will steady yourself and choose a firm foundation that makes it impossible for even the most difficult challenges to destroy love.

❧

> "Love one another deeply, from the heart" (1 Peter 1:22).

How can you choose love by *doing* love today?

Related Readings
Galatians 6:2; Ephesians 5:2; 1 John 3:23

46

When You Are Wronged, Mistreated, or Betrayed

The LORD will vindicate me; your love, LORD, endures forever—do not abandon the works of your hands.

Psalm 138:8

I bet there was a time when someone wronged, mistreated, or betrayed you. Perhaps someone stole from you, defamed you, or ruined your trust. In response, maybe you wanted to retaliate, to repay evil for evil against Christ's command (Romans 12:17). Maybe you wanted to show the other person "who's boss." But if that's the case, you must put away these ungodly motives and submit yourself to God's sovereign rule.

When you were wronged, perhaps you wanted to "win," which for you meant the circumstances would be resolved and justice would be done. Until then, you believed God couldn't bless you; His hands were tied from giving you favor because the other person seemed to have gotten away with what was unfair.

⁓

"[You] who saves me from my enemies. You exalted me above my foes; from a violent man you rescued me" (Psalm 18:48).

Listen up (*this is important!*): When injustices, betrayals, and mistreatments happen, you must redefine what it means to have God's favor. You don't have God's favor *only* when the situation is resolved or the other person is disciplined. You have God's favor *now* as you decide not to allow what the other person did—or is doing—control you or steal your joy, peace, or faith in God. This means you don't dream of retaliating, hold a grudge, stew, mope, or say bad things about your enemy to others, which only stirs up unholy vengeance. Instead, you place your life into the hands of your almighty, loving Father.

You must channel your anger over the injustice into prayer, into praise, into faith. You must choose to believe there is no person on the planet who can destroy you or the plans God has for you, because God reigns over your life and you are His precious child. The moment you believe the lie that other people have ruined you is the moment you give them power they were never meant to have.

✍

"He does as he pleases with the powers of
heaven and the peoples of the earth. No
one can hold back his hand or say to him:
'What have you done?'" (Daniel 4:35).

Do you believe God is with you? Are you confident He knows all and that He is faithful? Or are you giving your faith lip service? At the point you are mistreated is the point at which you must decide: "Is my faith real, or am I faking it? Will I believe God?"

Related Readings
Psalms 73:1-25; 84:11; Luke 12:32

47

Thoughts on Hearing God's Voice

He who is of God hears God's words.

John 8:47 NKJV

I once traveled into Chicago from our home west of the city by train. On the way, I didn't notice the clickety-clack of the tracks because I was engrossed in thought about hearing God's voice. The following ideas came to me and I wrote them down. I hope they encourage you.

If we know about God without being connected to God, Christianity will seem flat and empty, like it isn't real or authentic. Christians may seem like they are faking it, because at some level *we* are faking it; we aren't living in authentic relationship with Christ and we project onto the body of Christ what we feel ourselves. And speaking of relationship, that's something I have been thinking about too. In Christian circles, we throw the word "relationship" around a lot, don't we? Don't get me wrong, being a Christian is about relationship.

⁓

"I am the vine; you are the branches" (John 15:5).

But I find it so interesting that we can say we have a relationship with Jesus, but rarely talk with Him, and maybe even more rarely listen to Him. That would be like a woman saying she has a relationship with her husband but she rarely speaks to him and doesn't listen to a word he says. That's not a relationship. That's delusion. What we need is a redefinition of relationship. And part of that definition involves listening. Which, I might add, is exciting.

Few things in life are truly more thrilling than hearing the tender, sometimes convicting, always life-giving voice of God. I am not talking about a big, booming voice that comes out of the heavens. But instead, a still, small, quiet voice that meets you in your quiet place as you read His Word and listen for Him. Those moments are some of the most amazing times anyone can experience in life. Personal connection with the Living God! Frankly, there is nothing better. And what could be more miraculous than the God of the universe reaching out to speak to His creation? The immortal connecting with the mortal.

“My sheep hear My voice, and I know them, and they follow Me; and I give eternal life to them, and they will never perish; and no one will snatch them out of My hand” (John 10:27-28 NASB).

Are you listening?

Related Readings
John 10:14; 1 John 5:20; Revelation 3:20

48

When You're Waiting on God to Reveal His Plan

He has made everything beautiful in its time. He has also set eternity in the human heart; yet no one can fathom what God has done from beginning to end.

Ecclesiastes 3:11

Many of us have times when we want to know God's plan, but He isn't revealing it. We wrestle in prayer and in the silence of God. We anguish over an answer not yet given. This can feel discouraging, especially when we know He has the ability to reveal His will to us. We know He could give us a vision or a dream, speak to us through a friend, or cause a message from Scripture to burn in our hearts so brightly we can't deny His desire.

But we must remember that, in the silence of God, He is concerned not just with the answer we seek, but with our transformation. He wants us to be fully ready to receive His truth. Therefore, His revelations are perfectly timed. In John 16:12-15, Jesus told His disciples this very thing when He said:

> I have much more to say to you, more than you can now bear. But when he, the Spirit of truth comes, he will guide you into all truth. He will not speak on his own; he will speak only what he hears, and he will tell you what is yet to come. He will glorify me because it is from me that he will

> receive what he will make known to you. All that belongs
> to the Father is mine.

Clearly, Jesus wanted to reveal His secrets to His disciples. He wanted to bless them with the knowledge He had received from His Father. But He *needed* to reveal it to them at the appropriate time, when they were ready to receive His words.

Ellicott's Commentary on the Whole Bible says:

> On [Jesus's] side there is readiness to impart to them as friends all that He heard from the Father. But revelation can only be made to the mind which can accept it; and for those who have only in part understood what He has told them, there are many, many things which cannot now be borne.[12]

This is a great encouragement to us as we wait on God to reveal His will. In His great love, He reveals His truth at the perfect time, when we are ready to receive it.

⁓

"With many similar parables Jesus spoke the word to them, as much as they could understand" (Mark 4:33).

Are you willing to wait on God until the perfect time for Him to reveal His plans to you?

Related Readings
Matthew 13:34-35; 1 Corinthians 3:1-2; Hebrews 5:11-14

49

At the Crossroad of Love and Self-Protection

Greater love has no one than this: to lay down one's life for one's friends.

John 15:13

We all sometimes stand at the crossroads of love and self-protection, when we can choose self-sacrifice and selflessness or comfort and selfishness. This is when love requires great courage. These crossroads can come during relational conflict, when health problems or financial worries strain a relationship, or when we aren't sure if the love we give a child, grandchild, friend, mate, neighbor, or coworker will be returned.

During these times, we must remember that when Christ calls us to love, we need to follow His example of courage in Romans 5:8: "God demonstrates his own love for us in this: While we were still sinners, Christ died for us."

Jesus loved sinners. He loved those who wouldn't return His love. He loved those who would break His heart. He demonstrated courageous love. When He stood at the crossroads of love and self-protection, He chose love. Christ was also able to love selflessly and avoid the trap of self-protection because He lived to please His Father. He lived to do the will of the One who sent Him (John 4:34).

Last year I stood at the crossroads of love and self-protection. For part of a day, I chose self-protection. Then I remembered Jesus loved because He entrusted Himself to His Father and that love requires courage. Sure, it would have been easier to run to protect myself from rejection. But when I decided to make it my goal to obey Christ's call to love just as Christ obeyed His Father, rather than focus on my fears and feelings, my anxiety subsided, my courage grew, and my compassion for those He was calling me to love increased.

Jenifer Fox wrote, "Loving someone with no promise of any return is a sacred kind of love."[13] Indeed it is, because it takes faith. It takes being willing to follow Christ's example to lay down your life. It takes a courageous heart. When God calls us to love, we must remember we don't love primarily for our benefit or for the benefit of the object of our love, but for Jesus. Sometimes we must choose love simply out of obedience.

⚬◦⚬

> "A new command I give you: Love one
> another. As I have loved you, so you must
> love one another" (John 13:34).

When God is calling you to love and you are standing at the crossroads of love and self-protection, will you follow Christ's example?

Related Readings
Romans 12:10; Philippians 2:3; 1 John 3:16

50

When My Sister and I Heckled Our Neighbor

*Peace I leave with you; my peace I give you. I do
not give to you as the world gives. Do not let
your hearts be troubled and do not be afraid.*

John 14:27

Many of us have memories we are not proud of. I have one from
my elementary school years. When I was six, my sister and I
huddled behind the bushes next to our front porch and unabash-
edly heckled the woman across the street as she cuddled on the front
steps with her boyfriend. "First comes love, then comes marriage, then
comes the baby in the baby carriage!" We chanted—and screamed—
until she probably wanted to march across the street and twist our ears.
I don't remember much except that she was a young, single mother of
a newborn son who was trying to make ends meet while she lived with
her parents. I wonder if our chanting ever made her think, "Yes, I know
the order of things, except that it just didn't turn out that way for me."

Life is often like that, isn't it? We know how things *should* go. We
know how we would have liked our life to turn out like a fairy tale. But
no matter how we try to arrange for what we want, life often doesn't
go how we plan—maybe because of our own sin, someone else's sin,
or just because we live in a world adamantly opposed to God's ways.

"In this world you will have trouble. But take heart!
I have overcome the world" (John 16:33).

When life doesn't turn out the way we'd like, we have two choices: we can either believe God can redeem our story with His grace or we can demand our own way and live in torment. If we choose the latter, we will end up holding nothing but our tears. The way to healing in the midst of life that has gone awry is always surrender. For the young woman who sat on the doorstep, it's true that she didn't get her "First comes love, then comes marriage, then comes the baby in the baby carriage," but God hadn't finished writing her story. She went on to marry a young man who became a father for her son. God loves to rewrite tragedies into triumphs. With Him, there is always hope for something better.

crs

"We know that in all things God works for the
good of those who love him, who have been
called according to his purpose" (Romans 8:28).

Do you believe God can make something beautiful of your difficult story?

Related Readings
Romans 8:35-39; James 1:12; 1 Peter 5:10

51

Is Love in Your Equation?

*In Christ Jesus neither circumcision nor
uncircumcision has any value. The only thing that
counts is faith expressing itself through love.*

Galatians 5:6

I haven't taken any math classes since I was 14 years old because equations give me a rash. But I recently read an equation that moved me. For three days, it rolled around in my head and forced me to take a serious look at how I have often defined success.

I discovered this convicting equation in a book titled *Spiritual Simplicity* by Pastor Chip Ingram. As the basis for his equation, Chip evaluates the popular Scripture, 1 Corinthians 13:1-3, which says:

> "If I speak in the tongues of men or of angels, but do not have love, I am only a resounding gong or a clanging cymbal. If I have the gift of prophecy and can fathom all mysteries and all knowledge, and if I have a faith that can move mountains, *but do not have love, I am nothing.* If I give all I possess to the poor and give over my body to hardship that I may boast, *but do not have love, I gain nothing*" (emphasis mine).

Chip writes, "Paul's goal in this passage was to help the church of Corinth focus on what matters most. In helping them deal with misplaced priorities, he gives the Corinthians one overarching principle as a guideline to help them determine what's really important. His guideline was simple, yet profound: *anything minus love is nothing.*[14] Or, in a simple equation: *Anything – love = nothing.*

Let that sink in. Even *good* things—like "speaking in the tongues of men or of angels," or having gifts of prophecy and faith—if they are minus love, are nothing. *Absolutely nada. Zero. Zip. Zilch. A big goose egg in God's eyes.* This truth hit me hard as I took a long look at my motives for why I do what I do. My career minus love = nothing. My ministry minus love = nothing. My dreams minus love = nothing. And all my other good deeds? Minus love they are nothing. God defines success as L-O-V-E. That means everyone can be successful, because everyone can express love.

"Now that you have purified yourselves by obeying the truth so that you have sincere love for each other, love one another deeply, from the heart" (1 Peter 1:22).

Are the best aspects of your life motivated by what God defines as success—LOVE?

Related Readings
1 Corinthians 13:8; Galatians 5:22; Colossians 3:14

52

God Doesn't Talk Like Mom

*Oh, the depth of the riches of the wisdom and
knowledge of God! How unsearchable his
judgments, and his paths beyond tracing out!*

Romans 11:33

My mom talks in details. She won't only tell you she purchased fabric for her latest quilt; she'll tell you *why* she purchased the fabric, *who* she was with at the store, *when* she bought it, and *how much* it cost. She might say something like, "You know Mary? She's the lady with the schnauzer. Anyway, I went shopping with her today and I purchased some fabric from the store around the corner from her house. Well, the fabric has a blue background with an orange pattern. I just love patterns. Anyway, the fabric was on sale, $2.99 per yard. Great deal!"

In years past, I wished God was more like Mom, that He would give more details to answer my questions, specifically about the future and my direction. Because I didn't feel loved by Him, I didn't feel safe. I was certain more knowledge would mean more control without the possibility of ruining my life. After years of frustration and reasoning and worrying too much, I finally rested more in God's love so I was able to stop demanding I know everything about His plans for me.

⌒∂⌒

"See what great love the Father has lavished

on us, that we should be called children of
God! And that is what we are!" (1 John 3:1).

I realized how much I had matured in this area when I read some of my old journals. I saw that, over and over, I thought God was doing a particular thing in my life, but it turned out He wasn't doing that at all. I didn't have a clue what was going on and He worked it out—*without my help*! I'm thankful I no longer feel the same fear-driven desire to know everything about my life in advance.

David knew how to let go of the details and let God deal with them. He quieted himself when He didn't have all the answers about the future. He let God be God. If you're worrying today, choose, like David, to let God be in charge—without giving you all the details.

༄

"I do not concern myself with great matters or things
too wonderful for me. But I have calmed and quieted
myself; I am like a weaned child with its mother; like
a weaned child I am content" (Psalm 131:1-2).

Are you able to rest in the knowledge that God loves you, even though He doesn't give you all the details about the future?

Related Readings
Deuteronomy 29:29; Job 11:7-9; Psalm 139:6

53

When You Feel as Though You Don't Fit In

*But our citizenship is in heaven. And we eagerly
await a Savior from there, the Lord Jesus Christ.*

Philippians 3:20

In his book *Soul Cravings*, Erwin Raphael McManus writes, "Home is ultimately not about a place to live but about the people with whom you are most fully alive. Home is...about community and belonging, and we are all searching for home."[15]

Indeed, God has created us with a desire to belong. We have a need to know we are part of a larger whole. But the reality is sometimes we don't feel like we fit in. We may feel as though someone or something put us outside a circle everyone else is standing in while we look on from the outside. We may feel like we don't belong.

"They were foreigners and strangers
on earth" (Hebrews 11:13).

If you feel as though you don't fit in, let me offer you this encouragement: Could it be your Creator, who loves you, intentionally and strategically placed you "outside the circle" because He wants you to do something great for Him? Remember, being set apart for greatness sometimes means being set apart from the status quo. You can't influence the world and be like the world. Focusing on this truth will turn your feelings of not belonging into thoughts of purpose and privilege.

You are different from others because God made you different on purpose, for His purposes. Remember Noah? He was different from and rejected by his neighbors because God gave him a purpose that required him to be different. There must have been times when Noah felt like an outsider, *but he was an insider with God.* Remember Moses? When those he led into the Promised Land argued with him and stood against him (Exodus 17:3), he must have felt like an outsider. But he was exactly where he needed to be because he was fulfilling God's plans. Sometimes you can't do what everyone else is doing and be like everyone else, and still fulfill God's plans and purposes for you. Dare to be different for God.

"We are God's handiwork, created in Christ
Jesus to do good works, which God prepared
in advance for us to do. (Ephesians 2:10).

How does it make you feel when you reframe your uniqueness within the context of being set apart to do something special for God?

Related Readings
Ephesians 2:19; 1 Peter 1:17; 2:11

54

Live Like Someone Left the Gate Open

The Spirit God gave us does not make us timid,
but gives us power, love and self-discipline.

2 Timothy 1:7

Sometimes you need to build a gate to keep something out, and sometimes you need to build a gate to keep something in. The latter was the story at our house a few weeks ago. You see, our dog, Dixie, loves to play—which is why she has left the confines of our yard several times and come back with a tennis ball, probably belonging to some poor dog now deprived of playing fetch. One morning after disappearing into our neighborhood, where few houses have fences, Dixie came back with a whole bagel that was hard as a rock. She dropped it at my feet as if to say, "C'mon, play with me."

So after five tennis balls and a bagel, we decided a gate on our deck would keep her home. Now she spends her afternoons sunning herself on the deck.

This experience with Dixie made me think about my life with God. Sometimes I have lived like Dixie, full of courage to move beyond the comfortable to do great things for Christ. Other times I have lacked the faith that would take me to the edge for Him.

"Without faith it is impossible to please God,
because anyone who comes to him must
believe that he exists and that he rewards those
who earnestly seek him" (Hebrews 11:6).

I recently listened to a message by Francis Chan, who said when we are children, we often believe God is so big, so amazing, and so powerful, that He can do anything. So we are willing to risk for Him. We are willing—and even excited—to live like "someone left the gate open."

But then as we age, maybe we experience a few failures and get discouraged. Or we listen to others who tell us to be more realistic or more responsible. So courage takes a backseat to comfort and faith is shoved aside. Let's remember that God rewards courage because courage always translates into faith.

"I love those who love me, and those who
seek me find me" (Proverbs 8:17).

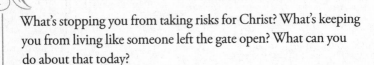

What's stopping you from taking risks for Christ? What's keeping you from living like someone left the gate open? What can you do about that today?

Related Readings
Romans 8:15; Ephesians 1:5; 1 John 4:18

55

The Power of Leading Your Heart with Truth

Search me, God, and know my heart; test me and know my anxious thoughts. See if there is any offensive way in me, and lead me in the way everlasting.

Psalm 139:23-24

I recently heard some great advice: Emotions are like children. It's okay to let them ride in the car with you, but don't let them in the driver's seat. Oh! What if we always remembered to judge between emotions that, if we follow them, will lead us down a good path and those that could lead us down a destructive path? What if instead of allowing our emotions to lead us we chose to lead our hearts with truth? Can you imagine how different the world would be?

Couples wouldn't allow emotional offenses to drive a wedge between them. Spouses wouldn't be driven by deceitful desires to commit adultery. Neighbors wouldn't allow hate to cause them to repay evil for evil. People wouldn't give up on their dreams when they should stay the course. Men wouldn't run into shopping malls and shoot innocent people. Friends wouldn't allow anger to rule over them during a disagreement. Oh! How would it be if we always remembered to lead our hearts with truth rather than allow our emotions into the driver's seat of our lives?

> "Guard your heart above all else, for it determines
> the course of your life" (Proverbs 4:23 NLT).

When your emotions are screaming, "Give up!" but you know quitting would be disobeying God, you've got to lead your heart with truth. When your feelings are telling you, "You're a loser," you've got to lead your heart with truth rather than believe that lie. When your heart is saying God doesn't love you, no one will accept you, you're useless, you're a failure, that it's okay to hate, hold a grudge, commit adultery, repay evil for evil, run from God, or abandon hope, you've got to lead your heart with God's truth so you can stay on His good path for your life. You must lead your heart with the truth found in the Word even when your heart doesn't feel like the truth is true. And the way to lead your heart is to spend time with Christ and learn of Him.

⌁

> "Then you will know the truth and the
> truth will set you free" (John 8:32).

Do you need to submit your emotions to God and allow Him to transform them with His truth?

Related Readings
Psalms 26:2; 119:105

56

Dealing with Difficult People

*"Do not be overcome by evil,
but overcome evil with good."*

Romans 12:21

In the Christian life, it's easy to say yes to what seems so good. *Yes, Lord. I receive that blessing! Yes, Lord. I'll give you that burden. Yes, Lord. I'll marry that wonderful man!* But some yeses are difficult, like, *Yes, Lord. I'll forgive.* And *Yes, Lord. I'll pray for my enemy* (or that person who is driving you crazy).

I once read 2 Timothy 2:26, where Paul tells Timothy to gently instruct those who oppose him "that they will come to their senses and escape from the trap of the devil." The word "devil" in this sentence reminded me things are often not as they seem because there is a spiritual realm we can't discern, and that people can be taken captive by the devil to do his will. Immediately Ephesians 6:12 came to mind:

> For our struggle is not against flesh and blood, but against the rulers, against the authorities, against the powers of this dark world and against the spiritual forces of evil in the heavenly realms.

Is it time to get your eyes off the one you see as your adversary and identify your *real* adversary? Moving your gaze from flesh and blood to a recognition that there are evil powers and forces you can't see in the spiritual realm can transform you from a blamer and finger pointer aimed at the wrong target to a righteous pray-er who does battle for Christ.

When life throws us a difficult relationship, it's easy to focus solely on the person who seems to be causing our problems. But if we want to do spiritual battle for Christ and foil the Devil's schemes to stir up trouble, isn't the superior alternative to say yes to prayer? What if we turn the tables on Satan and come against him for the benefit and freedom of the difficult person in our lives? One of my Facebook friends said it best: "Note to self: My adversary is in need of my prayers for deliverance, [he or she is not in need of] my anger, bitterness, and resentment."

"But I tell you, love your enemies and pray for those who persecute you, that you may be children of your Father in heaven" (Matthew 5:44-45).

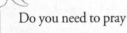

Do you need to pray for a difficult person in your life? If so, do it now.

Related Readings
Matthew 5:44; Luke 6:27-28; Hebrews 12:1

57

How Fear Can Make You Stronger

Don't be afraid; just believe.

Mark 5:36

In his book *Fearless*, Max Lucado writes, "Can you imagine a life with no fear?" My answer to Mr. Max's question is, "No, I can't imagine it, but I *can* imagine making fear work for me so it makes me stronger."

Does the idea of fear strengthening you sound absurd? The truth is when you leverage fear it can be a great help in your relationship with God. Instead, it can be the very reason you become a stronger woman and more of who God designed you to be. Fear does not have to be a bad thing; you just have to know what to do with it. If you listen to your fear, it can be a great teacher. Here's why: it will show you where you have holes in your shield of faith and where you aren't believing God. Remember, fear and faith cannot co-exist.

"There is no fear in love. But perfect love drives out
fear, because fear has to do with punishment. The one
who fears is not made perfect in love" (1 John 4:18).

When you understand why you aren't believing God and the reason for your fear, the fear that was meant to destroy your faith can be used to strengthen your faith—and your determination.

Let's say you are afraid of starting a new women's Bible study.

Leverage your fear for greater faith by asking the Lord, "Why am I afraid? What's causing it?" Seek Him. Ask Him to speak to you through His Word and the Holy Spirit to show you what's behind your fear. For example, He may reveal to you that you are afraid because you are afraid of failure. After God reveals to you why you are afraid, ask Him to show you His truth through Scripture and the Holy Spirit. One truth He may show you is that you can do all things through His strength (Philippians 4:13). This is how fear, the very thing that could paralyze you, is the very thing that can make you stronger. Again, fear does not have to be a bad thing; you just have to let it drive you to the One who can set you free from fear.

⁓

"Why are you so afraid? Do you still
have no faith?" (Mark 4:40).

Are you afraid of the future, of what might or might not happen? Don't allow fear to paralyze you; let it push you to seek God's truth so it will make you stronger.

Related Readings
John 14:27; Romans 8:15; 1 John 4:12

58

Is It Time to Zip Your Lips?

Out of the heart come evil thoughts.

Matthew 15:19

My mother is the Queen of Phrases. One of her favorites I heard as I was growing up was "Zip your lips" whenever I was speaking and shouldn't have been. Ephesians 4:29 is also about doing a little lip zipping: "Let no corrupt communication proceed out of your mouth, but that which is good to the use of edifying, that it may minister grace unto the hearers" (KJV). In the NIV, this Scripture says, "Do not let any unwholesome talk come out of your mouths, but only what is helpful for building others up according to their needs, that it may benefit those who listen." In *Barnes' Notes on Ephesians-Philemon*, the word "unwholesome" in this passage is the word *sapros* in the original New Testament Greek and it means "bad, decayed, rotten, and is applied to putrid vegetable or animal substances."[16]

Perhaps we want to label this Scripture as "optional" because gossip, slander, lying, harsh words, insults, sarcasm, and ridicule aren't as bad as murder and adultery, and other "bigger" sins, right? Wrong. God takes the sins we commit with our mouths just as seriously as "bigger" sins because all sin comes from the heart. So when we break this command not to let any unwholesome or corrupt talk come out of our mouths, we have failed to love God and love others, which are His two greatest commandments:

> Jesus replied: "Love the Lord your God with all your heart and with all your soul and with all your mind." This is the first and greatest commandment. And the second is like it: "Love your neighbor as yourself." All the Law and the Prophets hang on these two commandments (Matthew 22:37-40).

Ephesians 4:29 reveals we can be a blessing with our mouths but we can also hurt others with our speech. Our communication can even corrupt others. (That's pretty powerful, isn't it?) We can actually contaminate people with the words we speak. So we must ask ourselves, "Is my speech building up or tearing down those who listen? Am I giving them the gifts of courage and hope, holiness, and faithfulness through my words, or do my words reveal my pride and selfishness? Are my words a blessing or a curse?"

⟡

"We take captive every thought to make it obedient to Christ" (2 Corinthians 10:5).

Do you need to ask the Lord to help you take your thoughts captive so your speech is gracious?

Related Readings
Galatians 5:19-2; Colossians 3:5-7; 1 Peter 1:14-15

59

When You Want to Give Up Before You Start

I am the LORD, the God of all mankind.
Is anything too hard for me?

Jeremiah 32:27

Have you ever had an idea that set your soul on fire? You were sure God was calling you to do something for Him and you were totally stoked. You immediately wrote down your idea and told your best friend. But then a couple of hours or days passed and the flame of enthusiasm you initially felt began to die, doused by the reality of what it would take: resources you didn't have, courage you felt you lacked, and expertise you didn't possess. So because it looked impossible, you gave up before you started.

This common scenario reminds me of when Nehemiah, in the book of Nehemiah, describes how he rebuilt the wall of Jerusalem. His passion for this project was ignited when he asked one of his brothers, Hanani, about the Jewish remnant that had survived the exile. Hanani said, "Those who survived the exile and are back in the province are in great trouble and disgrace. The wall of Jerusalem is broken down, and its gates have been burned with fire" (Nehemiah 1:3).

This meant Jerusalem was defenseless against her enemies. When Nehemiah heard this, he was deeply moved, so he sat down and wept. For "some days" he mourned and fasted and prayed before God. Finally, his passion led him to petition God for favor in approaching the king to ask for help in rebuilding the wall.

Sadly, some of us never get past the passion stage where Nehemiah was during his "some days" of fasting, weeping, and praying for favor from the king. Sure, we may pray for days or weeks when an idea has set our souls on fire. But then we take inventory of what following our desire will require and what we lack, and before we know it we have talked ourselves right out of moving forward. We determine it would be best to stop wanting and dreaming and instead just stick with what's safe—even if it will kill our hearts. We dry our tears, brush off deep emotions that could lead us to action, and decide we won't move forward because it's just too risky. Don't you think it's tragic that we give up before we have taken even one step toward what could be God's plan?

ॐ

"[Jesus said], 'With man this is impossible, but with
God all things are possible'" (Matthew 19:26).

Are you not pursuing your God-given dream because you are focused on the obstacles?

Related Readings
Job 42:2; Jeremiah 32:17; Psalms 3:8; 62:11

60

Nothing You Give Up for Christ Will Be Lost

*For whoever wants to save their life will
lose it, but whoever loses their life for
me and for the gospel will save it.*

Mark 8:35

In 2012, before I married, God called me to relocate to a city far from my family. I was excited about the opportunity to serve, but I also felt some grief. I had moved so many times over the years that being close to family had become more important to me.

When the Lord made the move clear, first I cheered with excitement. I was confident God was leading me to uproot and, like Abraham, to go. And then I cried. Afterward, He took me to Mark 10:29-30:

> "Truly I tell you," Jesus replied, "no one who has left home
> or brothers or sisters or mother or father or children or
> fields for me and the gospel will fail to receive a hundred
> times as much in this present age…and in the age to come
> eternal life."

This Scripture reminded me that God notices all the work we do for Him and that those who know Christ will be rewarded in heaven for what they do on the earth. For example, 1 Corinthians 3:12-15 says our earthly works will be tested by fire and that if what we have done (or built) survives, then we will receive a heavenly reward. Isn't it awesome that God, who is a good Master, will pay back those who belong to Him for works well done after they go home? He takes nothing from the Christian without making multiplied restoration in a new and glorious form.

When I embrace these truths, difficulties take on eternal meaning. I am bolstered with confidence that nothing in this world can really shake me because nothing I give up for Christ will ever be lost. Every sacrifice will be ultimately redeemed. Joy! In Christ, we win and the story ends very, very well.

An internal freedom comes when we realize that what we do here matters for forever, and because it matters for forever, absolutely no earthly happening will ever be able to destroy us. Nothing will ultimately ruin us. No disappointment will keep us down—and nothing we give up for Jesus will be lost. In light of heaven, it joys me to know that the loved ones I said good-bye to will always be with me and we can spend eternity catching up on what I missed. In the end, we win. No matter what you are giving up for Christ, know that He notices and you will be rewarded.

❧

"Store up for yourselves treasures in heaven, where
moths and vermin do not destroy, and where
thieves do not break in and steal" (Matthew 6:20).

Does having an eternal perspective help make the pain of surrendering things and people you love easier?

Related Readings
1 Corinthians 9:23; Hebrews 11:24-26; Revelation 2:3

61

Why Saying No Can Bless the One Who Opposes You

Peter and the other apostles replied, "We must obey God rather than human beings!"

Acts 5:29

When I first felt God calling me to become a writer, I was ecstatic. But not everyone shared my enthusiasm, including my mom. She felt I needed to earn more money, so she suggested I take another career path. I now realize if I had done what Mom asked, I would have missed out on seeing God work in so many amazing ways—and Mom would have missed it too. Some time ago she told me, "My faith has grown as I have watched the Lord provide for you."

My experience reminds me of what transpired between Ruth and Naomi in the book of Ruth. When Naomi's husband and two sons died, she was left alone with her widowed daughters-in-law, Ruth and Orpah. Naomi left Moab with her daughters-in-law to go back to Bethlehem, to her people. But then she *urged* Orpah and Ruth to go back to their home because she thought that was best for them. Orpah did turn back, but Ruth clung to Naomi and urged her not to tell her to go away. Then Ruth made a promise to Naomi when she said:

> "Don't urge me to leave you or to turn back from you. Where you go I will go, and where you stay I will stay. Your people will be my people and your God my God. Where

you die I will die, and there I will be buried. May the Lord deal with me, be it ever so severely, if even death separates you and me" (Ruth 1:16-17).

Ruth's conviction led her to go against her mother-in-law's urging. As a result, Ruth went to Bethlehem with Naomi, where she later met and married Boaz, and together they had a son. As a wonderful end to this tragic story, Naomi's family—and hope—were restored. Can you imagine what Naomi would have missed if Ruth had taken her advice rather than follow her conviction?

Is someone urging you to do what they believe is best for you even though it goes against what God is calling you to? Could it be that saying yes to them would mean saying no to blessing them later as they witness God's work in your life?

"Then a teacher of the law came to
him and said, 'Teacher, I will follow you
wherever you go'" (Matthew 8:19).

Isn't it liberating to remember that our first priority is to follow the Lord and He will take care of the rest?

Related Readings
Luke 14:33; 1 Corinthians 1:20; 3:19

62

The Big Red "S" Bus

*Speaking the truth in love, we will grow to
become in every respect the mature body
of him who is the head, that is, Christ.*

Ephesians 4:15

S in is like a big bus with an *S* on the side. If I notice a Christian brother or sister is going to run into the road in front of it, am I loving them if I just say, "Hey, it's all going to be okay. You're doing great!"? Is it loving to remain silent if I know they are going to ruin their marriage, destroy their career, hurt their body, devastate their children, or make a mess of their finances?

Many times I have had a sinful attitude and made some pretty stupid decisions. Even though it would have been difficult for me, I wish a mature, faithful, Christian friend who loved me would have talked with me. I needed someone to help me work through what I was feeling so I could get my heart right with Christ.

⁓

"Wounds from a friend can be trusted, but an
enemy multiplies kisses" (Proverbs 27:6).

I fear being politically correct has become the enemy of Christian virtue and loving others. Maybe you've heard people say, "It's not my place to judge." True, we can't judge someone's salvation. But we are to judge—or identify sin—so we won't be deceived. In John 7:24 Jesus says we are to make "righteous judgment" (NKJV).

Galatians 6:1 says, "Brothers and sisters, if someone is caught in a sin, you who live by the Spirit should restore that person gently. But watch yourselves, or you also may be tempted." How can we see someone "caught in sin" if we don't judge sin? Jesus also says in Luke 17:3, "If your brother or sister sins, rebuke them, and if they repent, forgive them." Of course, I am not advocating beating up people with a "holier than thou" critical attitude. We are called to love in humility (Matthew 7:5). But we must realize loving someone and "rebuking" them if they are caught in sin as Christ commands are not polar opposites. They are one and the same. It's helping them so they don't get flattened by the big *S* bus.

⌒

"God disciplines us for our good, in order that we
may share in his holiness" (Hebrews 12:10).

Whom can you trust to faithfully tell you the truth when you need it? Are you a faithful friend who will speak the truth to keep others from destruction?

Related Readings
John 13:35; James 1:5,13-15

63

God Uses Ordinary People Just Like You

*His pleasure is not in the strength of the
horse, nor his delight in the legs of the warrior;
the LORD delights in those who fear him, who
put their hope in his unfailing love.*

Psalm 147:10-11

Maybe, like me, you struggle with fully depending on God. As I pondered this problem one afternoon, I wrote the following words in my journal. I hope they are an encouragement to you.

Self-sufficiency is the enemy of grace. If we believe we are able to do everything on our own, why do we need God? Our inadequacies are an opportunity for Him to show Himself sufficient. In this there is grace, a gift we could never receive if we could solve our own problems.

God's grace, and therefore His power, isn't made manifest in those who believe they have no need for help. It doesn't shine most brightly in the "I-can-do-it-myself" types. It shines in the inadequate, in those who know they need God's power to succeed and endure. It shines when we are unable to pull ourselves up by our bootstraps. This is when He can show up to do great things in our impossible

131

situation. This is when He is glorified and we are strengthened in our faith and hope by watching Him work.

&

> "But God chose the foolish things of the world to shame the wise; God chose the weak things of the world to shame the strong…so that no one may boast before him" (1 Corinthians 1:27-29).

He moves in—and through—ordinary people. He always has and always will. And because that is true, one of the most powerful acts we can do is thank God for what we cannot do on our own and then invite Him into our inadequacies. When we do, He provides grace to sustain, equip, and guide us for the road ahead. God's grace is sufficient, because when you are weak then you are strong (2 Corinthians 12:10).

To receive the gift of grace that brings with it God's enabling power to accomplish His plans and purposes, we must humble ourselves and admit that we are unable, dependent, and that without Him we can "do nothing" (John 15:5).

&

> "If I must boast, I will boast of the things that show my weakness" (2 Corinthians 11:30).

Will you invite Christ into your inadequacies and thank Him that you are able to do all He calls you to do through His grace and power?

Related Resources

Psalm 8:2; 1 Corinthians 1:20; James 2:5

64

A Lesson on Anger from Peanuts

Do not be overcome by evil,
but overcome evil with good.

Romans 12:21

In *Betrayed by God? Making Sense of Your Expectations*, I wrote about the struggle that many of us have with anger. Perhaps you can relate.

At my former job, I hung a poster outside my cubicle showing Lucy from Peanuts screaming, "Look out everybody! I'm gonna be cranky for the rest of the day!" Lucy's announcement became a joke with my co-workers because she's so not like me. Somewhere in my youth, I learned that anger was unacceptable, possibly because I often saw it misused. Then when I came to Christ, this faulty message was reinforced in church. After all, good Christian boys and girls never get angry, right? Wrong. Not only is this teaching wrong, but God expects that we'll experience anger. God never said "Don't ever get angry," but He did say...

"In your anger do not sin" (Ephesians 4:26).

This Scripture acknowledges that people get angry. Why? Because anger is a secondary response to emotional pain. And there's no doubt there's a lot of emotional pain to go around on this sin-filled planet! Anger will happen! Anger is like a red light on the dashboard of a car signaling that something is wrong under the hood—that there's a hurt that needs to be given to God and perhaps forgiveness granted to someone. Like desperation, anger has the potential to take us to places of deeper intimacy with Christ when we bring what hurts us to Him for healing. How can you do this? Yell or scream when no one is around or run outside and holler at the universe. You can also do what author Muriel Cook calls "Hot Pen Journaling." Write down your true emotions without sweetening it. Be real. Tell God the truth. Then ask Him to show you what's fueling your anger so He can minister to what's hurting you through prayer and His Word.

Several years ago I was angry when someone I loved hurt my feelings. Rather than denying how I felt or sinning by taking it out on someone, I beat up my bed. I yelled. I screamed. I clobbered it as hard as I could. The result? I felt 100 percent better. I forgave the person who wounded me and thanked God for loving me. A short time later I was singing a song, proclaiming His truth and praising His name.

"Behold, You desire truth in the inward parts, and in the hidden part you will make me to know wisdom" (Psalm 51:6 NKJV).

Will you trust God with your most honest and vulnerable emotions today—even anger?

Related Readings

Psalm 37:8; Proverbs 19:11; Ecclesiastes 7:9

65

When You Wonder Why God Hasn't Answered Your Prayer

*They who wait for the L*ORD *shall renew their strength;
they shall mount up with wings like eagles; they shall
run and not be weary; they shall walk and not faint.*

Isaiah 40:31 ESV

Because I didn't walk the aisle of matrimony until I was 46, I sometimes wondered why God wasn't answering my prayer for a mate. Now that I have found my Mister, I can see some of the reasons it took some time for me to marry.

I am convinced that the years of my life from 30 to 46 were for ministry and I had to be single to do much of what God led me to accomplish. Second, I would not have been ready for the man God brought me earlier. I had to make some mistakes along the way so I was open to a relationship with my husband.

∽

"We know that in all things God works for the
good of those who love him, who have been
called according to his purpose" (Romans 8:28).

This reminds me that sometimes we have to go through what we don't want to go through to get to what God wants and what is best.

During these times, surrender to God may be difficult. So, in the Lord's mercy, He may temporarily withhold an answer or revelation from us that would bring instant and clear perspective because we aren't ready for the answer, even if we think we are. He knows the perfect time to answer our prayer. It's only after we have waited and wrestled in confusion, and perhaps tried to do things our own way and fallen flat in failure, that our hearts have been made pliable in the process to receive God's answer.

In John 16:12, Jesus says, "I have much more to say to you, more than you can now bear." Jesus wanted to reveal more to His friends. He was willing to reveal more, but He could only do so at the proper time when they were ready. Maybe you are waiting for God to bring an answer and you wonder why it's taking so long. Remember, He loves you and He only gives the best to His kids. He knows the best time to answer.

಼ೂ

"He who did not spare his own Son, but gave him
up for us all—how will he not also, along with him,
graciously give us all things?" (Romans 8:32).

Are you open to patiently waiting on the Lord until it's the right time for Him to answer your prayer, even if you can't see why He hasn't answered?

Related Readings
Mark 4:33; John 15:15; Hebrews 5:11-14

66

My Graduation from Spiritual Kindergarten

As the body without the spirit is dead,
so faith without deeds is dead.

James 2:26

Over the last couple of years I have felt as though the Lord is inviting me to graduate from spiritual kindergarten, even though
I thought I had already received my diploma. As I have walked with
Christ for more than 20 years, my understanding has sometimes been
like that of many who have been told, "Just ask Jesus into your heart
and you'll go to heaven."

Yes, Romans 10:9 says, "If you confess with your mouth that Jesus is
Lord and believe in your heart that God raised him from the dead, you
will be saved" (ESV). However, it's been hitting me that confession is the
beginning of belief. Then comes discipleship. This is what it means to
follow Christ. Perhaps this is why Matthew 7:21 says, "Not everyone
who says to Me, 'Lord, Lord,' shall enter the kingdom of heaven, but
he who does the will of My Father in heaven" (NKJV).

Those are some heavy words. In this Scripture, we are reminded
that Christ isn't here to serve us; we are here to serve Him. And it's not
just about saying we believe while we live our own lives. It's sobering...
Jesus asks those who know Him to *live for Him*—and nothing less.

We must remember that yes, we are saved by grace. We can't do anything to earn our way into heaven (Ephesians 2:9). But we must also remember that faith without works is dead (James 2:20). In any relationship—including the one with Christ—action doesn't prove love, but true love is *always* proven by action. That said, all works for Christ begin with the motivation of the heart in relationship with Jesus or they are just dead works. The condition of our heart is central to discipleship. Is God asking you as He has been asking me, "Will you follow Me, or will you say you believe but still do your own thing?" Is it your turn to take God more seriously and graduate from spiritual kindergarten?

> "Many will say to Me on that day, 'Lord, Lord, did
> we not prophesy in Your name, and in Your name
> cast out demons, and in Your name perform
> many miracles?' And I will declare to them, 'I
> never knew you'" (Matthew 7:22-23 NASB).

Has the Lord convicted you that your actions need to match your verbal affirmations of love for Him? Ask Him for the power to demonstrate your love.

Related Readings
1 Corinthians 15:58; Hebrews 4:11; 12:1

67

Only God Gets to Be the Cake

*Everyone who has been born
of God overcomes the world.*

1 John 5:4 ESV

I once heard a woman say she wanted another child. "I know another child will make me happy," she said. She already had eight. I imagine she discovered Number 9 couldn't do anything for her that Numbers 1–8 hadn't. It seemed this woman had made an idol out of motherhood. I used to think an idol was either an icon, like those I see in a particular shop window near my home, or something you owned that also "owned you." But I later realized an idol can be anything you *want* more than God, something you believe will "save" you—just like this woman believed another baby would save her.

Somewhere in my thirties, it dawned on me afresh that all my brightest dreams fulfilled, and even the greatest gifts life offers—such as the love of a good man, good family, and good friends—would never fully satisfy. That's because fulfilled desires are the icing on the cake of life, not the cake. And they can never be the cake. It's not possible. Only God gets to be the cake. It's the way He designed His relationship with us.

"You shall have no other gods before me" (Exodus 20:3).

When we admit that all the things we want the most cannot fill us, we are in a *very good place*. At first, it may make us feel desperate because we come face-to-face with our emptiness. But it's a good kind of desperate because it can lead to peace and rest. Until then, we are like girls who scream in a panic as they grasp at the sky, "I want!" But once we admit nothing in this world can satisfy like Christ, we can lie down in the gentle grass of God's enough. And then (Ah, joy!) comes rest from striving.

To realize you are desperate and that nothing in this world can satisfy leads to liberation from the bondage of serving idols that never keep their promises. All of us have a choice: we can admit nothing in this world will ultimately fill us, or we can spend our entire lives on an endless chase of emptiness, running after one desire after another for satisfaction—and be miserable.

ొ

"Do not love the world or anything in the world. If anyone loves the world, love for the Father is not in them" (1 John 2:15).

Do you believe anything in life will satisfy besides Christ? Talk to Him about your desires and ask Him to help you love Him most.

Related Readings
Romans 12:2; Colossians 3:1-2; James 4:4

68

Liberating Grace and the Power of "I Can't"

*From his fullness we have all received,
grace upon grace.*

John 1:16 ESV

Our society is all about "I can." I can win the race. I can be the best salesperson in my company. I can get a college degree. I can be a good mother. We have been taught that the most important things can be earned if we only believe and try hard enough. Certainly, when God is behind something, all things are possible for him who believes (Mark 9:23). But there is an "I can't" phrase every believer needs to embrace: I can't earn God's love. This phrase is empowering, liberating, and life-giving. Granted, most believers know they are "saved by grace through faith" (Ephesians 2:8) so they intellectually agree that salvation can't be earned. They will also *say* His favor and love can't be earned. But there is often a disconnect between what we *say* we believe and what we truly believe.

For example, in his book *Holiness by Grace*, Bryan Chapell shares that many people believe that if they have a quiet time, God will love them more. If they are kind to their neighbor, it's a guarantee of His favor. "However much we may want—or feel the need—to trophy our good works before God in order to merit his acceptance, our accomplishments remain insufficient to obligate him to care for us as members of his family."

❦

> "But if it is by grace, it is no longer on the
> basis of works; otherwise grace would
> no longer be grace" (Romans 11:6).

So what *does* guarantee God's care and unfailing love? Only His goodness and the covenant He made through Christ's sacrificial death on the cross. It's not anything we do. When you are in Christ, there is nothing you can do to make Him love you less and there is nothing you can do to make Him love you more. He just loves you. That's it. His love is unchanging, unshifting, secure, steadfast, and unalterable. What great news!

Knowing you can't earn God's love will liberate you from the bondage of perfectionism and from the fear that God will reject you when we get to heaven because you haven't been good enough. And it will free you to serve Him with a thankful heart, secure in His steadfast love the way a well-loved child is secure.

❦

> "I am convinced that nothing can ever separate
> us from God's love" (Romans 8:38).

Are you convinced that you can't do anything to earn God's love—that His work on the cross was sufficient to grant you favor with God?

Related Reading
Romans 6:14; 3:20-24; Ephesians 2:1-10

69

Getting Older

We do not lose heart. Though outwardly we are wasting away, yet inwardly we are being renewed day by day.

2 Corinthians 4:16

When I turned 40, I went through a time of transition. Rather than taking off to Walmart without make-up as I have always done, I turned into the clone of a 17-year-old girl, only with a few more wrinkles and a lot more antiaging cream. Also like a teen, I started primping, fixing, smoothing, and shaping, and wondered what I would do when I turned totally gray. During this season, the deterioration of my physical body felt like a huge emotional burden as the world's message, that only the young and physically perfect are valuable, weighed heavily on my middle-aged ego. I called a girlfriend to ask if she was feeling the same. "Oh, boy! I can relate!" she said. My question sparked a half-hour discussion about floundering through the transition to life's middle years.

After a few months of quietly grieving the loss of the past, God revealed something beautiful to me about waving good-bye to physical youth: even though the deterioration of our earthly bodies often feels like a hindrance, it is a priceless gift, a gift that reminds us that this life is passing away—and that heaven is a reality.

*"Set your minds on things above, not on
earthly things" (Colossians 3:2).*

Therefore, the passing of time is God's personal invitation to focus on what is truly important, such as developing a stronger relationship with Him and living with intentionality and purpose.

Some people who are deeply impacted by the loss of physical youth finally follow the dreams God placed in their hearts years before. Some decide the career they have been chasing now needs to take a back-seat to a calling to serve God and others in a new way. Unfortunately, women—and men—who insist on holding on to the past as they age may fall into the world's ways of worshiping youth, rather than taking care of their relationship with God and being a blessing to others. They may fall prey to sacrificing the relationships dearest to them as they try to recapture the past. However, when we have a godly perspective, there is nothing like the stripping away of our physical props to enlarge our hearts to what is truly valuable and never changes.

⁓

*"Jesus Christ is the same yesterday and
today and forever" (Hebrews 13:8).*

Are you grieving the loss of physical youth? Determine to focus on what is eternal and can never be lost.

Related Readings
Matthew 16:23; Luke 12:15; John 2:15

70

When You Feel Caught in the Mundane

If anyone gives even a cup of cold water to one of these little ones who is my disciple, truly I tell you, that person will certainly not lose their reward.

Matthew 10:42

I think most women have felt caught in the mundane. We're changing our baby's diaper, attending a dance recital, or writing up what feels like a meaningless report. Some tasks just make us feel like we're making little impact. If these sentiments resonate with you, you are in good company. I have been there too! But here's great news: you can rise above feelings of futility. It's just a matter of redefining what you do from God's perspective.

In his book *66 Love Letters,* Dr. Larry Crabb provides an encouraging reminder for everyone who has wondered if their work matters. "Nehemiah did little more than build an unimpressive wall around an apparently insignificant city [Jerusalem] that has a relatively small population of unimportant-looking people. And yet, when people laughed at him for taking on such a trivial project, he replied, 'I am doing a great work' (Nehemiah 6:3)."

As if God is speaking, Crabb goes on to write,

> Whatever anyone does out of a sincere desire to know me
> and draw others to me is a great work. And as you engage

in work, sometimes you will be energized as you catch a glimpse of my plan unfolding. More often you don't. Either way you are doing a great work.

Every father who repairs a leaky faucet and then prays with his kids before dinner is doing a great work. Every mother who prepares that dinner and joins in prayer is doing a great work. Every single person who works hard to pay the rent and reads the Bible before bedtime is doing a great work. I see it all. And I am pleased. Their reward is coming.[17]

Indeed, He sees and knows it all (Psalm 139:1-6). The great news is when we truly believe God knows all and sees all and that it all matters to Him, we will be motivated to do our work with excellence. We can also experience the joyful reality that every good work is a great work when it's done for Christ.

⁓

"The King will reply, 'Truly I tell you, whatever you did for one of the least of these brothers and sisters of mine, you did for me'" (Matthew 25:40).

What did God see in your day today that made Him smile?

Related Readings
Proverbs 19:17; Galatians 5:22; 1 Peter 1:22

71

Just Get Busy

*As we have opportunity, let us do good to all people,
especially to those who belong to the family of believers.*

Galatians 6:10

I love it when God hits me over the head with something I need to learn by presenting the same truth to me several times. This happened when I saw Ephesians 5:15-16 in three different places in one day. It says, "Be very careful, then, how you live—not as unwise but as wise, making the most of every opportunity, because the days are evil."

"Okay, Lord, I understand we are to make the most of every opportunity, but what does 'the days are evil' mean?" In search of an answer, I found a couple of commentaries and came up with the following treasure from Albert Barnes: "Because the days are evil, because the times in which you live are evil, there are many allurements and temptations that would lead you away from the proper improvement of time... and that would draw you into sin...to go places where time would be wasted."[18]

"Whatever you do, work heartily,
as for the Lord" (Colossians 3:23 ESV).

As I read this quote, I felt I had been caught up in the allurements of too many questions about what I should do. "Lord, should I speak at another event or not? Should I start another radio program?" It was as if the Lord was reminding me, "Stop wasting time by getting immobilized and paralyzed by your feelings and fear. Just get busy for Me. I will guide you as you move forward and work. You don't have an unlimited amount of time."

I once knew someone who spent years agonizing over how she was supposed to serve God. She sat at home doing nothing as fear led her into inactivity. In the meantime, time to serve God was a wastin'.

When we spend our days languishing in indecision, we can spend so much time wondering *what* we should do for Christ that we do little. We must remember that eternity is closing in, and that we have only a limited amount of time to make a difference. We have numerous opportunities to serve Christ and others in our churches, neighborhoods, and workplaces. We just have to keep our eyes open.

∽

"As long as it is day, we must do the works
of him who sent me. Night is coming,
when no one can work" (John 9:4).

Do you need to be more mindful to notice the opportunities to serve Christ right in front of you each day?

Related Readings
Romans 13:11; Galatians 6:10; Ephesians 6:13

72

Loved Despite Your Imperfections

God is love.

1 John 4:16

Have you noticed we may say we love a job, a new car, a hat, or the song on our iPod? We may even tell an acquaintance "Love ya" or say we are in love. And love and sex are often confused.

With all these mixed messages about love, it can be difficult to understand the real meaning of love. According to the Bible, there is no greater love than the love expressed through Christ and His sacrifice on the cross.

⌘

"Greater love has no one than this: to lay down
one's life for one's friends" (John 15:13).

In his book *The Ragamuffin Gospel,* Brennan Manning tells a story from Dr. Richard Selzer, MD, who visited a couple after a surgery during which he had to remove a tumor from the wife's cheek. The story is a touching illustration of Christ's love for imperfect people like me and you.

"I stand by the bed where a young woman lies, her face post-
operative, her mouth twisted in palsy, somewhat clownish.
A tiny twig of the facial nerve, the one to the muscles of her

mouth, had been severed. She will be this way from now on. I had followed with religious fervor the curve of her flesh; nevertheless, to remove the tumor in her cheek, I had to cut the little nerve. Her young husband is in the room. He stands on the opposite side of the bed and together they seem to dwell in the evening lamplight, isolated from me, the moment is a private one. Who are they, I ask myself. *He and this wry mouth I have made, who gaze at each other so generously, so lovingly?* The young woman speaks. 'Will my mouth always be like this?' she asks. 'Yes,' I say, 'it will. It is because the nerve was cut.' She nods and is silent. But the young man smiles. 'I like it,' he says, 'It's kind of cute.' All at once I know who he is. I understand and I lower my gaze. One is not bold in an encounter with a God moment. Unmindful, he bends to kiss her crooked mouth and I am so close I can see how he twists his own lips to accommodate to hers, to show her that their kiss still works."[19]

In love, the Perfect God bent to kiss imperfect humanity. You are wholly loved by God despite your imperfections.

∽

"See what great love the Father has lavished on us, that we should be called children of God!" (1 John 3:1).

Do you believe God's truth that you are wholly loved?

Related Readings
John 1:12; 3:16; Romans 5:8; 8:37-39

73

Dare to Dream Again

*I am the LORD, the God of all mankind. Is
anything too hard for me?*

Jeremiah 32:27

Have you noticed that little girls know how to dream? If you ask any elementary-school cutie patootie what she wants to be when she grows up, she'll probably give you a list as long as her list for Santa. When I picked up a friend's five-year-old daughter from school one afternoon, she told me she wants to be a ballerina, play the clarinet, play the piano, be an artist, be a scientist, do math, be a teacher, be a writer, play the flute, and do "house stuff." House stuff, I discovered, meant actually building houses and giving them to the poor—a daring goal for such a tiny girl!

Ask most adults what they wanted to be when they were little, and they will say they wanted to be a biologist, a nurse, or an actor. Ask them what they want to be now, and they might say, "I always wanted to be a biologist, but…" "I always wanted to be a nurse, but…" "I always wanted to be an actor, but…"

❧

"With God all things are possible" (Matthew 19:26).

Somewhere between 5 and 25 many of us stop believing anything is possible—even with God. We lose our childlike wonder and shove down the very desires that could be the whispers of Christ inviting us to take our place in His greater story.

Those who live with the faith of a little child listen to their longings and allow them to tug them toward what seems impossible. They do not numb their desires by looking too much at future obstacles or say, "But it's not financially possible," or "But I don't have the talent," or "But my family wouldn't approve," or "But I don't have the time." Instead, they let their desires speak, filling up their hearts with the possibility of "What if?" So they step out in faith even when they don't have the plan fully mapped out. They know if their dream starts with God, then God will fulfill the dream.

"Truly I tell you, anyone who will not receive
the kingdom of God like a little child
will never enter it" (Mark 10:15).

Imagine you are five years old again. You are sitting in the backseat of my car when I ask you, "What do you want to be when you grow up?" What do you say?

Related Readings
Jeremiah 32:17; Isaiah 64:8; Luke 18:27

74

Is It Time to Raise Your Gaze Above Your Troubles?

See, I have refined you, though not as silver; I have tested you in the furnace of affliction.

Isaiah 48:10

A couple of years ago my husband and I faced a cross-country move because of a job change. We wrestled with many of the decisions that come with relocation and starting over in a new life. I was concerned about many things. Would I make friends? Would we find a church we'd love? Would my husband like his new job? After a few months, I started to wonder if sometimes we are too focused on *what happens* to us when God is most concerned with *how we respond to what happens to us.* Don't get me wrong. Jesus cares about all our needs, but perhaps our experiences aren't just about the experiences—about liking our jobs, making friends, or finding a good church. Instead, they are opportunities and tests to learn and become more like Christ.

Because eternity is part of the believer's reality, no pain we experience will ultimately wound. No trial will last forever; no marital trouble, financial difficulty, romantic loss, or family devastation will matter after we die.

"God shall wipe away all tears from their eyes;

and there shall be no more death, neither
sorrow, nor crying, neither shall there be
any more pain" (Revelation 21:4 NKJV).

But what will matter is how we responded to what happened to us because every response is shaping—or not shaping—the character of Christ in us and affecting others around us. We focus on the temporal; God is concerned with the eternal. Our Christlikeness here on the earth will echo in the halls of eternity. It will affect forever. So maybe we need to raise our gaze a little higher above what happens to us to *how we respond to what happens to us.*

ᘜᘜ

"[Trials] have come so that the proven genuineness of
your faith—of greater worth than gold, which perishes
even though refined by fire—may result in praise, glory
and honor when Jesus Christ is revealed" (1 Peter 1:7).

Are you going through a difficult time? How can you look at your trouble through the lens of eternity so it affects your now and positively affects the good you do during hardship?

Related Readings
Romans 12:12; James 1:2; 1 Peter 4:12

75

Great Expectations

*You, Lord, are our Father. We are the clay, you are
the potter; we are all the work of your hand.*

Isaiah 64:8

One of my good friends often says, "Never put a period where God puts a comma." It's her way of reminding herself to stay flexible to God's rule and to submit to His sovereignty over her life. This can be especially difficult when we've got big plans or hopes that have led to great expectations.

Expectations can be awesome. They have the potential to bring us great joy when fulfilled and focused energy when we need to complete a particular task. They also have the potential to usher in great disappointment when they are dashed. It's then that we must remember to "never put a period where God puts a comma." We must submit to His will if we want to live with joy. To continue to demand our way only leads to internal death.

꿈

"Woe to those who quarrel with their Maker, those
who are nothing but potsherds among the
potsherds on the ground. Does the clay say to the
potter, 'What are you making?' Does your work
say, 'The potter has no hands?'" (Isaiah 45:9).

Many times my expectations haven't lined up with God's will. And when the pain of unfulfilled expectations pierced my heart, I wanted to shut down hope, silence expectations, and never dream again. But a better way is to surrender to Christ in faith. *Surrender doesn't mean giving up; it means giving in.* It means giving Him control. We put our plans in His hands as we work. We give Him our children as we raise them. We surrender the outcome of our job search as we look. And when things don't go as we planned, we do not live as those who have no hope, those who start telling themselves, "Don't dream because you'll just be disappointed." No, we remember God has a plan—and it's always a good plan—even if it's not our plan.

❧

"Trust in the LORD with all your heart and lean not on
your own understanding; in all your ways submit to him,
and he will make your paths straight" (Proverbs 3:5-6).

Do you believe God has a good plan even if it's not your plan?
Talk with Him about this today.

Related Readings
Psalms 62:8; 147:3; Jeremiah 17:7-8

76

How God Surprised Me

*Delight yourself in the Lord, and he will
give you the desires of your heart.*

Psalm 37:4 ESV

Have you prayed about and desired something for a very long time, maybe even years? Have you hoped for it so long you have doubted God will ever answer? Maybe in your quiet—and honest—moments you have felt overlooked by Christ. And perhaps you have even given up hope He will ever grant your desire.

I can relate. I felt the same before I married. I had been praying for over two decades for a husband. I am still amazed that God chose to answer my prayer in an unexpected way—and definitely much later than was comfortable. But I am not disappointed. In fact, I am grateful, filled with joy, and in awe because I am seeing Christ in a new way. Through God's delayed answer—and His creative way of fulfilling my desire—I received a fresh glimpse of His glory and power demonstrated through His redemption. I am convinced more than ever that He loves to take what is horrible, tangled up in sin, and seems to be permanently broken, and redeem it so He is glorified. And as a result, we are *delighted*. In the surprise of His unexpected redemption, we see His magnificence, His glory, His love, and His power in ways we wouldn't if life fit the fairy tale we had designed for ourselves.

"The heart of man plans his way, but the Lord
establishes his steps" (Proverbs 16:9 ESV).

Through God's delay and unexpected way of answering my prayer for a mate, He has helped me see in a greater way that He is good—even when our biggest dreams do not come true how we want. And He has taught me that the most amazing blessing is not in receiving the perfect life of our imaginations. It is not getting everything we think will make us happy. Instead, it is knowing Him and experiencing His love. *This trumps every trouble.*

I am so very glad my story did not turn out as I had designed it in my mind. For this very reason, I am learning to love more deeply and less selfishly, not in spite of things not turning out how I wanted, but *because* things didn't turn out how I wanted. And in this, there is overwhelming joy.

∾

"Hope deferred makes the heart sick, but a desire
fulfilled is a tree of life" (Proverbs 13:12 ESV).

How have you seen God's redemption in your story even though it hasn't been written the way you would have chosen?

Related Readings
Proverbs 15:29; Psalms 91:15; 145:19

77

You've Got to Lead Your Heart

*As obedient children, do not conform to the evil
desires you had when you lived in ignorance.*

1 Peter 1:14

As a new Christian I was a sensitive, creative type, and I was extremely driven by my emotions. I couldn't grasp how something could be true if it didn't feel true. This mind-set made believing God difficult.

I once came across a great book that revealed how my emotions led me to doubt God, even after I became a follower of Christ. In his book *Roll Away Your Stone*, Dutch Sheets shows the difference between our souls—which are made up of mind, will, and emotions and are called the *psuche* in the Greek New Testament—and the spirit (*pnuema*). Sheets writes, "When you are born again, your spirit is instantly renewed, but it's a different story with the soul."[20] Our spirits become new creations (2 Corinthians 5:17) and are made complete in Him the minute we come to Christ (Colossians 2:10). But our souls (mind, will, and emotions) are still driven by worldly ideas, rebellion against God's truth, and seduction by Satan's lies. Perhaps this is why Scripture says, "Do not conform to the pattern of this world, but be transformed by the renewing of your mind" (Romans 12:2).

Therefore, when I live by my feelings, I'm being driven by my unredeemed soul rather than by God's truth. A wise woman lives by faith and by what God says, *not* by what she feels. Granted, this doesn't mean we're unfeeling, but our feelings are governed by truth. Our faith overcomes our feelings. In his book *The World's Last Night and Other Essays*, C. S. Lewis writes, "Feelings come and go, and when they come, good use can be made of them: they cannot be our regular spiritual diet."[21] Those who let feeling rule the day will, as I did, find themselves in a spiritual ditch.

In the movie *Fireproof*, while trying to convince the main character, Caleb (Kirk Cameron), not to leave his wife, Caleb's friend says, "Don't just follow your heart, because your heart can be deceived. You've got to lead your heart." Indeed, we must lead our hearts with God's truth, because feelings can be untrustworthy.

❧

"If anyone is in Christ, the new creation has come: the old has gone, the new is here!" (2 Corinthians 5:17).

Will you make the choice to believe God today despite how you feel?

Related Readings
Ezekiel 36:26; Ephesians 4:21-24; James 4:4

78

Filling in the Blanks of God's Promises

They will have no fear of bad news; their
hearts are steadfast, trusting in the LORD.

Psalm 112:7

Have you noticed love can make women act wacky? For example, when a young woman is smitten with a young man, she may interpret the most insignificant of his actions as a sign of mutual affection. Maybe she hears from a friend he is coming to the church potluck. "Oh, that must mean he's hoping he'll run into me!" she thinks. She sees him at a festival and he glances her way. "He must feel the same way I do!" She runs into him after not seeing him for weeks. "I remember you," he says. This time she thinks, "He must like me because he remembers me!" The desire to receive love can be so strong that it will cause us to "fill in the blanks" with answers to our desires. Believe me, I've been there!

Sometimes we do something similar with God. A desire can be so strong, that we "fill in the blanks" of His promises. For example, the Lord reveals a particular thing He is going to accomplish in our lives. He has promised to give us children, move us across the country, or provide a new career. We believe what He says and we are excited, but then we make the mistake of "filling in" the blanks of what God said with promises He never gave.

✑

"Blessed is the one who trusts in
the LORD" (Jeremiah 17:7).

We will become a mother of exactly five boys and two girls. He will move us across the country to a city near our family. He will give us a new career where we'll be making twice as much as before. We need to be careful not to add on to what God said lest we become discouraged and blame Him for not fulfilling "promises" He never made.

When "blanks" or unanswered questions about what He has promised or what He is going to do in the future concern us, we can hold firmly to the certain promises He *has* given. His love and affection for us are fixed. He will always do what is absolutely best for us, and His perfect holiness demands the perfect handling of all that concerns us. You can trust Him with all you can't see ahead. You don't need to "fill in the blanks."

✑

"Trust in the LORD with all your heart, and
lean not on your own understanding; in all
your ways acknowledge Him, and He shall
direct your paths" (Proverbs 3:5-6 NASB).

Have you ever "filled in the blanks" of God's promises? If so, what was your motivation?

Related Readings
Psalm 51:10; Ezekiel 11:19; Hebrews 13:5

79

A Late-Night Conversation with a Lesson

The boundary lines have fallen for me in pleasant places; surely I have a delightful inheritance.

Psalm 16:6

One year as my husband and I reflected on our long Thanksgiving weekend with our family, we talked about the moments that had blessed us most. We made Christmas cookies and decorated the tree. We sang songs, celebrated my stepdaughter's birthday, went out to eat, played games, painted Christmas ornaments, acted younger than our ages, and stayed up way too late. We even played touch football in the rain and mud and attempted a game called Groundies, which I am sure has been popular on playgrounds everywhere among elementary schoolchildren. We'd had too many blessed moments to count. But one simple memory is precious to me: a late-night conversation with my 19-year-old stepson, Brett.

After everyone else had gone to bed, we shared words in the kitchen over my cup of tea and a bag of popcorn. After talking about the numerous challenges life has thrown at both of us in the last few years, our conversation turned to focusing on the blessings in life.

"Everyone has a reason to believe their life stinks," I said. "Everyone has experienced something that could make them feel like they have been cheated. But there are blessings everywhere. Now because of what you have gone through, you are holding a gift in your hand you weren't holding before. You can use this gift to encourage others. Now when someone comes to you with a story that sounds a lot like yours, you can say, 'That happened to me, too, and here is what God did in my life.'"

"Yes," Brett said, "blessings are everywhere. You just have to choose to seek them out."

✑

> "This is the day which that the Lord has made; Let
> us rejoice and be glad in it" (Psalm 118:24 NASB).

Indeed. Wise words. You just have to choose to seek them out. And that, I believe, is a main difference between those who live victoriously in the face of trouble, disappointments, and dashed dreams and those who do not.

✑

> "How abundant are the good things that you have
> stored up for those who fear you,
> that you bestow in the sight of all, on those
> who take refuge in you" (Psalm 31:19).

Will you choose to seek out the blessings in your life today?

Related Readings

Isaiah 64:4; Habakkuk 3:17-18; 1 Corinthians 2:9

80

Battling a Critical Spirit

Brothers and sisters, do not slander one another.

James 4:11

Lately I have been convicted about the ungodly words that sometimes come out of my mouth. I have been asking God to give me gracious speech because I want to be a gracious woman. I have also been considering how gossip and picking people apart are sometimes treated as tolerable, "lesser" sins. After all, they're not as bad as murder, theft, adultery, or just about anything else on the Ten Commandments "thou shalt not" list, right?

God doesn't see it that way. In fact, James 3:6 describes the tongue, from where cursing others comes, as "a world of evil," "set on fire by hell," and with the ability to corrupt "the whole body." (Whoa! Let those thoughts sink in.)

James 3:9 says, "With the tongue we praise our Lord and Father, and with it we curse human beings, who have been made in God's likeness. Out of the same mouth come praise and cursing. My brothers and sisters, this should not be."

This should not be for a lot of reasons, and I imagine you and I could come up with a huge list of reasons—many more than I have space for here. But for now, let me give you just a few thoughts to chew on: Gossip, slander, and a critical spirit are robbers. Consider the amount of productive time that can be wasted if we spend it gossiping and picking people apart. Not only that, but cultivating a critical spirit robs us of time for what we should really be doing for others: praying.

Can you imagine how different the world would be if we channeled all the time and energy we spend gossiping and criticizing into prayer? Can you imagine what spiritual mountains we could move? Can you imagine how powerful we could be for the kingdom, winning over even our enemies to fight on our side of the spiritual battle? Can you imagine how all of eternity could be altered? Oh! What we forfeit when we spend our lives speaking negatively of others instead of fighting for their spiritual well-being!

"God opposes the proud, but gives grace
to the humble" (James 4:6 ESV).

Are you guilty of having a critical spirit? Do you enjoy pointing out the faults of others? Have pride and hatred entered your heart and are they showing up in your speech? If so, confess your sin to God today.

Related Readings
Ephesians 4:31; James 5:9; 1 Peter 2:1

81

What Might You Regret Not Doing?

All people are like grass, and all their glory is like the
flowers of the field; the grass withers and the flowers fall.

1 Peter 1:24

A couple of years ago, I visited my family in Idaho for Christmas. Two days before I was scheduled to board a flight back to my home in Georgia, I received a call from a friend. During our conversation he asked, "Is there anything you will regret not doing if you don't do it before you leave?" His question helped me prioritize the next 48 hours. "Yes," I responded. "Visit my grandmother. See my niece and nephew one more time." "Great!" he said. "Do those things."

After we spoke, it hit me hard that because time is limited, I should always live intentionally, not just when I am leaving my family. James 4:14 says, "What is your life? It is even a vapor that appears for a little time and then vanishes away" (NKJV).

According to this Scripture, the path of your life is quickly heading straight toward eternity. Every day you are moving closer—and you never know when it will be your turn to meet the God who made you. A friend of mine recently died unexpectedly in an automobile accident. She was 33 years old. She had no idea she would go home to heaven so soon. My grandfather died from a heart attack when he was only 58. He didn't know he would meet his Maker before his grandchildren were grown.

If you know Christ, one day you will also pass from here to eternity and join other believers who have gone before you. Like everyone, you never know when it will be your turn. For that reason, live intentionally, with the eyes of your heart focused on heaven and God's will for your life. In the same way that my friend asked me a question to help me live with purpose, let me ask you: If you knew you were going to die tomorrow, what would you regret not doing? Would you wish you had reconciled with an old friend? Spent more time with your loved ones? Followed a dream that God placed in your heart? Worked less? Loved more? Adventured more? Served God with greater devotion? Don't leave words unsaid or deeds undone today. You don't know what the future holds. Time is limited. Live intentionally. Eternity is ahead.

"Be careful how you walk, not as unwise men but as wise, making the most of your time, because the days are evil" (Ephesians 5:15-16 NASB).

What do you need to do *today*?

Related Readings
Matthew 7:12; John 8:12; 12:35

82

When Someone You Love Leaves

The Lord is close to the brokenhearted and
saves those who are crushed in spirit.

Psalm 34:18

As I was growing up, my mother taught me many valuable truths. For instance, every situation has a positive side; everyone has a right to their opinion; and too much talk can keep a problem stirred up. But I had to learn one thing she didn't teach me the hard way: sometimes people you love will leave. This is one of those difficult lessons most of us come face-to-face with in life.

Sometimes people leave because they can't love, sometimes because they feel guilty about themselves, sometimes because they are afraid of intimacy, and sometimes because God has another plan for you and they can't go where you are going. Sometimes they leave because relationships have their seasons, and sometimes because God removes them from your life. (That's His love and protection!) People leave for numerous reasons, but no matter *why* they leave, it's important to remember God loves you and their departure doesn't have to mean the end of your joy. Jesus never stops doing good for His kids.

"I remain confident of this: I will see the goodness
of the Lord in the land of the living" (Psalm 27:13).

There will always be people who *need* your love. The key is keeping your heart open—free from unforgiveness, bitterness, or self-hatred—and not becoming negative about people or cynical about love. It's tragic how we wound ourselves by making unhealthy vows not to love or trust again because someone abandoned us.

In his book *The Four Loves*, C. S. Lewis writes, "To love at all is to be vulnerable. Love anything and your heart will be wrung and possibly broken. If you want to make sure of keeping it intact you must give it to no one, not even an animal. Wrap it carefully round with hobbies and little luxuries; avoid all entanglements. Lock it up safe in the casket or coffin of your selfishness. But in that casket, safe, dark, motionless, airless, it will change. It will not be broken; it will become unbreakable, impenetrable, irredeemable. To love is to be vulnerable."[22]

In the aftermath of the disappointment of desertion, remember to guard against hardness of heart and ask God to give you His perspective about your loss. Keep your heart open so you can continue to love well. It will mean the difference between internal life and death.

❧

"He heals the brokenhearted and binds
up their wounds" (Psalm 147:3).

Are you afraid to love again? If so, pour out your heart about it to the Lord.

Related Readings
Psalms 27:10; 55:13-16; Isaiah 40:11

83

The One Question That Changes Everything

*We know that for those who love God all
things work together for good, for those who
are called according to his purpose.*

Romans 8:28 ESV

I n an article titled "As the Lights Go Down," Nicole Kear tells about a visit she made to the optometrist's office when she was just 19 years old. What she thought would be an inconsequential eye exam turned her life upside down. As she walked home after her appointment, she couldn't believe the news. She was going blind due to a degenerative retinal disease, and was told she would probably completely lose her eyesight by the time she was 35 years old.

❧

"He causes His sun to rise on the evil and the
good, and sends rain on the righteous and
the unrighteous" (Matthew 5:45 NASB)

In the following weeks, Nicole felt she might buckle under the weight of the diagnosis. But she also started to appreciate little things she had never noticed before. Not only did she begin to notice beauty in a new way, but she realized she needed to make the most of her days.

"I could use the death sentence my eyes had been given as a kick in the pants to start *really* living."[23]

When life throws us a curveball, a natural first response is often to ask *Why?* But a better question to ask is *What? Why* will lead you down a dead-end path. *What* will lead you to action. "Lord, what do You want me to do for You?" "God, what's Your desire for me now?" "Christ, what is Your plan?"

When you ask *What* instead of *Why,* you take on the posture of a servant. This is where you find peace. Peace comes when you are in right relationship with your Maker. Those who discover how to live within the power of *What* instead of languishing in *Why* make their time on earth count. They do not waste their days looking backward; they spend them looking forward. They see themselves as a gift to others and as they ask Christ *What,* they find ways to serve. Their lives become vessels through which all of their experiences—good and bad—become fuel for great works to be performed. By partnering with God and through the power of the Holy Spirit, you can begin to live in *What,* rather than being held captive by the nagging unfruitfulness of *Why.*

⁂

"The LORD is my strength and my shield; in him my heart trusts, and I am helped; my heart exults, and with my song I give thanks to him" (Psalm 28:7 ESV).

Are you living in the power of *What?*

Related Readings
Psalms 30:11-12; 56:3-4; 84:11

84

Why So Many Relationships Fail

*Now that you have purified yourselves by obeying
the truth so that you have sincere love for each
other, love one another deeply, from the heart.*

1 Peter 1:22

When people have failed to love, perhaps they did not recognize this great flaw in their character because it was hidden behind blame as they made copious mental notes about the shortcomings of their beloved. These shortcomings led them to believe loving was impossible. "If only she wasn't so insensitive." "If only he was more complimentary." "If only she took better care of herself." "If only he was more supportive."

We must remember that this way of thinking is unwise. Another's flaws—and even sin—may stretch our love and make us feel like it's impossible to love, but another's imperfections are never justification for why we can't love. Love is a choice when the emotions of love fail us. Anything less is self-serving love. Certainly, in extenuating circumstances, someone's sin may prevent us from having a relationship with them, as is often the case in abuse, addiction, adultery, or abandonment. But sin and imperfections are never a justification for why we can't love with Christ's agape love, which means we love them with their best interest in mind.

"Do nothing out of selfish ambition or vain
conceit. Rather, in humility value others
above yourselves" (Philippians 2:3).

The great news is when the imperfections of those closest to us do their good work to refine us and make us more like Jesus, they drive us to our knees in supplication: "Lord, please help me to be less selfish! Teach me how to love!" But when we don't allow another's imperfections to illuminate our selfishness, inflexibility, and pride, their flaws can even become the reason we justify our ungodly actions of unfaithfulness, slander, divorce, or abandonment.

How tragic that we often blame to justify our own sin! And how equally tragic that it's often only after we have fallen for the Devil's seduction, shunning the wise warnings and counsel of others, that we may realize how we have been blinded by sin and have desperately wounded ourselves and those closest to us. If we are wise, we will remember that the sin and imperfections of those closest to us can expose, point to, and draw out the sins in our own hearts to keep us from destruction.

೧೦

"There is none righteous, no, not
one" (Romans 3:10 NKJV).

Are you keeping a watch over your heart so you are not deceived by selfishness?

Related Readings
Romans 12:10; Galatians 5:26; James 3:14-16

85

How to Find Fulfillment in What You Do

*So whether you eat or drink or whatever
you do, do it all for the glory of God.*

1 Corinthians 10:31

I often receive emails from women I have met online or at a conference. Frequently someone will ask, "How do I know what I have been created to do? How can I know how God wants to use me?"

Maybe you wonder why you are here too. Thankfully, there are signs that point to why you have been created. One way you can discover why is to take a look at your deepest desires. You were made to love; you desire love. You were made for health; you desire health. And you were made to achieve, so you desire to achieve. No one lies on his or her deathbed and thinks, "I am so glad I wasted my days." Instead, we long to do something significant with the time we have been given.

But here is something important: when the reason we want to achieve is to serve ourselves—or worship ourselves—we'll end up feeling very empty, even if we achieve what we want. But when our desire to achieve points us toward Christ, when it points us toward our priority purpose to love God, we'll experience joy.

"Jesus said to him, 'You shall love the LORD your

God with all your heart, with all your soul, and
with all your mind'" (Matthew 22:37 NKJV).

Some people believe if they could just discover why they are here
and do what God has called them to do, they will finally be fulfilled.
But lasting and deep fulfillment doesn't come from just fulfilling a purpose or even using your greatest gifts and talents. It comes from using
your gifts and talents and knowing for whom you are using them. It
comes from serving God through what you do.

The artist who paints a picture simply to paint or just to make
money will never experience the same joy as the artist who paints to
glorify her Creator. Glorifying and loving God gives meaning and
deeper joy to everything we do.

Why do you do what you do? Whether you are teaching children,
writing blogs, serving a meal, or making a business deal, do it for
God's glory.

Related Readings
1 Corinthians 12:1-31; 1 Peter 4:11

86

Experiencing Greater Relational Intimacy

This I command you, that you love one another.

John 15:17 NASB

In his book *Soul Cravings,* Erwin Raphael McManus writes eloquently about love. "We are most alive when we find it, most devastated when we lose it, most empty when we give up on it, most inhuman when we betray it, and most passionate when we pursue it."[24]

This reminds me of Paul's admonition to the Corinthians in 1 Corinthians 14:1 (ESV):

"Pursue love," he writes.

Wait a minute. Isn't love supposed to just find you, like you just "find" a hole in the middle of the street when you fall in? Sure, love may initially require little effort, but to experience deep, long-lasting, intimate love requires a passionate pursuit, just as Paul said. This passionate pursuit sounds vague, and for that reason it seems impossible. After all, what does it mean to pursue love? Most of us have never been taught about developing emotional intimacy with another human. We've learned how to tie our shoes, do algebra, balance a checkbook, and maybe change the oil in our car, but no one has ever taught us how to pursue love.

Here's one way to pursue it:

Just about every door on planet Earth has a key to open it when it's locked. I have a key for my car door, for the door of my home, and even for the door to my jewelry box. Intimacy is the same. One particular key opens the Intimacy Door in your relationships, and it's called the Key of Acceptance. Because intimacy means we allow another person to "see into" us and they allow us to "see into" them, we must use the Key of Acceptance. After all, no one wants to allow someone to "see into" their heart who is controlling, judgmental, critical, sarcastic, unforgiving, abusive, selfish, or just plain nasty.

So if you want others to open their hearts to you, you've got to give them a safe place to do so. While most of us may act like we're not afraid of anything, in the deepest part of ourselves, our hearts are tender, fragile, and generally fearful of relational pain. For hearts to thrive in intimacy, they've got to feel safe and accepted.

&

"Love is patient, love is kind. It does not envy, it does not boast, it is not proud. It does not dishonor others, it is not self-seeking, it is not easily angered, it keeps no record of wrongs. Love does not delight in evil but rejoices with the truth. It always protects, always trusts, always hopes, always perseveres. Love never fails" (1 Corinthians 13:4-8).

What changes can you make to give your loved one a safe place to be vulnerable?

Related Readings
Colossians 3:12-13; 1 Peter 4:8

87

When You Don't Want to Go

*If anyone comes to me and does not hate father and
mother, wife and children, brothers and sisters—yes, even
their own life—such a person cannot be my disciple.*

Luke 14:26

Each Sunday after church, my husband and I pile into the car and head to our favorite lunch spot. On the way, we talk about the sermon and share what part of the message hit us. This week, Acts 8:1 grabbed me right in the heart. "On that day a great persecution broke out against the church in Jerusalem, and all except the apostles were scattered throughout Judea and Samaria."

Can you imagine it? The Jews were *forced* to leave their homes in Jerusalem because of persecution. They didn't have a choice. They had been done wrong and they had to leave. The great news is that these faithful believers were like little spores—or seeds—sent into the world to share the love of Christ with those who had never heard.

*"Those who had been scattered preached
the word wherever they went" (Acts 8:4).*

When they were forced out of Jerusalem, I can't imagine they said, "This is awesome. Because of our persecution and scattering away from home, God is spreading the good news of salvation to all people." They couldn't have seen through the windshield what could only be seen through the rearview mirror. But they were obedient to share Jesus's love wherever they went and trust Him with their futures—even though it was somewhere that didn't feel like home.

This message speaks to my husband and me as we prepare to move away from Chicago just 18 months after we moved in. Even though our new assignment is noble, we can't help but feel a little like we're being scattered. But we remember that our lives are not our own, that we are not here to be served but to serve, and that there are people who need to know Jesus and His grace. So like the Jews and all believers, we are little seeds being sent into the world. Even though we can't see through the windshield what we will be able to see through the rearview mirror, we are choosing obedience over comfort.

∽

"Anyone who loves their life will lose it, while anyone who hates their life in this world will keep it for eternal life" (John 12:25).

Has God asked you to go where you don't want to go? Trust Him and choose to serve Him wherever He calls, even if it's somewhere that isn't comfortable or doesn't feel like home.

Related Readings
Psalm 73:25-26; Matthew 22:37; Acts 20:24

88

When You Feel Lonely

Jesus often withdrew to lonely places and prayed.

Luke 5:16

Everyone experiences loneliness. It's a common denominator in the equation of life. Our natural response is often to run from it or deny it by filling our lives with distractions. God has a better way. When we allow loneliness to do its redemptive work by embracing it, it can promote positive life change. Here's how:

Loneliness can enlarge our hearts to love. Ten years ago, my grandfather was diagnosed with leukemia. During the weeks before his death, he hugged tighter, smiled wider, and laughed more. Saying good-bye to those he cared for enlarged his heart to love—his greatest sorrow produced a greater virtue.

"We know that in all things God works for the good of those who love him, who have been called according to his purpose" (Romans 8:28).

In the same way, the sorrow of loneliness can be fruitful by causing us to ache for human connection. Without it, we would never marry, engage in friendships, or endure the numerous problems that are a natural part of intimacy. Think back to when you've felt most lonely. My bet is that you longed for a human connection. In short, loneliness enlarged your heart to love.

Loneliness can also open us up to a deeper knowledge of God's love when we get alone with Him. Sometimes when I'm lonely I fight my need to spend quiet time with Christ. Why? Because facing loneliness can feel threatening. However, I've learned that when I embrace my loneliness and simultaneously hold the hand of God, I don't fall into a pit of despair as I feared. Rather, I find His comfort.

What do we miss when we run from loneliness and refuse to invite God into it? Ironically, the pain we try to avoid can create an even greater inner chaos. For example, a friend of mine always has a packed social calendar. When he's not working, he's helping someone with a chore, watching a movie, or engaging in any number of social activities. Certainly, there is nothing wrong with his interests. However, using busyness to hide from loneliness is wrong. God calls us to live balanced lives where we are neither afraid of solitude nor of being with others.

❧

> "After he had dismissed them, he went up on
> a mountainside by himself to pray. Later that
> night, he was there alone" (Matthew 14:23).

Do you feel lonely today? God created you for connection with others and Him. Allow your loneliness to motivate you to reach out to someone and to God.

Related Readings
Deuteronomy 31:6; Psalm 91:15; Mark 1:35

89

A Story About Muddied Motives

Behold, You desire truth in the innermost being.

Psalm 51:6 NASB

In 2003, I started a writing and speaking ministry with the right motives. I wanted to serve God; I cared about making His name great. A few years later, it became more about marketing campaigns, reaching more people, and succeeding in a career than about pleasing Christ. I am not happy to admit that my motives got muddied with worldly ideals. God started pressing the issue of my motives. I felt Him calling me to a place of deeper commitment where I would be willing to die to my desires and take a long, hard look at why I was serving.

I did a study in Galatians and reflected on Paul's life. I was reminded Paul was called through revelation by Jesus Christ (Galatians 1:12). He received this revelation that he might preach the gospel to the Gentiles (Galatians 1:16). Paul did not receive a church membership or a certification from study. He received a call from Christ. It hit me: *Jesus is the prerequisite for all authentic service or ministry for Christ.*

✍

"Whether you eat or drink or whatever you do, do
it all for the glory of God" (1 Corinthians 10:31).

This challenged me. I wrote in my journal:

When the world's ways to make ministry better through this tactic, that program, that campaign means we lose the heart of ministry, which is Christ, then we have missed God's point. But it's not easy to keep Christ as the heart of what we do, is it? It's not easy because if it's all about Jesus (no matter where or how we serve) and it's not about soothing our ego, succeeding in our latest marketing campaign, or reaching more numbers, then we must face ourselves and die to our desire for our own glory. We must let God lead. Ouch! Our affections must be purified. And we have to ask ourselves, "Do I love what I am doing more than I love Christ? Is my affection for my purpose, or is it for Him?"

⁂

"Whatever you do, whether in word or deed, do it all in the name of the Lord Jesus, giving thanks to God the Father through him" (Colossians 3:17).

No matter what you have been called to—to sing, teach, design, or work in the world some other way—will you serve rather than choose to be served? Is the point of your purpose to serve yourself? Or do you desire to serve Christ?

Related Readings
Zechariah 4:6; Ephesians 5:20; 1 Peter 4:11

90

A Love That Will Not Let You Go

*See how very much our Father loves us, for he
calls us his children, and that is what we are!*

1 John 3:1 NLT

When I came to Christ, no one warned me that desires for the things of the world could still tug so strongly on my heart. I had no idea I would sometimes be tempted to worship many other things and stray from the only One who was worthy of all my praise. And no one told me how God would relentlessly chase me in spite of my fickle affections for Him.

His persistent pursuit of my heart has sometimes amazed me, and sometimes brought me to tears. The grace of God is mind-blowing when we consider how steadfast, unchanging, and faithful is His love, not because of how good we are, but because of how good He is.

⌇

"Long ago the LORD said to Israel: 'I have loved you,
my people, with an everlasting love. With unfailing
love I have drawn you to myself'" (Jeremiah 31:3 NLT).

In Scripture, God's gracious love pursuit despite our sin is demonstrated in His relationship with Israel, an adulterous nation who served other gods and practiced pagan religion. Like my heart—and perhaps yours—can sometimes be, Israel was unfaithful to a love that would never let her go, but God still pursued.

The third chapter of Jeremiah is a beautiful example of this chase of love. Four times, in 15 verses, God says, "Return to me" to His people, after they have wandered and committed adultery with other gods and other loves. Only a man who really loves his wife asks her to come back so many times after she has repeatedly cheated on him. This is the kind of love the Lord has for us. It's the kind of love He has for *you*. If you've recently found a greater love than God in work, a relationship, money, ambition, possessions, or approval, He is saying, "Return to Me." He longs for you to come back home to Him. There is no criterion for your return, only an honest and genuine desire to renew your relationship with Him and a contrite and repentant heart. Won't you let Him be your all?

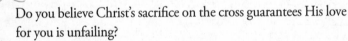

"Can a mother forget her nursing child? Can she feel no love for the child she has borne? But even if that were possible, I would not forget you!" (Isaiah 49:15 NLT).

Do you believe Christ's sacrifice on the cross guarantees His love for you is unfailing?

Related Readings
Hosea 11:4; Ephesians 2:4-5; Titus 3:4-5

Notes

1. Timothy Keller, *Counterfeit Gods* (New York: Viking, 2009), 29, 38–39.

2. *The Complete Word Study New Testament,* (Chattanooga, TN: AMG Publishers; Reissue edition June 1, 1991).

3. Timothy Keller, *The Meaning of Marriage* (New York: Penguin Books, 2013), 130–31.

4. *The Complete Word Study Old Testament* (Chattanooga, TN: AMG Publishers; Reissue edition June 1, 1994).

5. Webster's Dictionary, http://www.merriam-webster.com/dictionary/privilege.

6. *The MacArthur New Testament Commentary,* (Chicago, IL: The Moody Bible Institute of Chicago, 1983), 96.

7. C. S. Lewis, *The Problem of Pain/A Grief Observed* (Nashville, TN: Broadman & Holman Publishers, 1999), 26.

8. *The Life with God Bible* (New York: Harper One, 1989), 531.

9. Erwin Raphael McManus, *Soul Cravings* (Nashville, TN: Thomas Nelson, 2006), 23.

10. Michael Kendrick, *The Fulfillment Factor* (self-published, 2013), 56.

11. Keller, *The Meaning of Marriage,* 111.

12. Charles J. Ellicott, *Ellicott's Commentary on the Whole Bible Volume VI*: The Four Gospels (Wipf and Stock Publishers, 2015), 516.

13. Jenifer Fox, "Being a Mother Is Nothing like I Thought It Would Be," *Huffington Post,* 10/25/13, http://www.huffingtonpost.com/jenifer-fox/being-a-stepmother-is-nothing-like-i-thought-it-would-be_b_4160092.html

14. Chip Ingram, *Spiritual Simplicity* (Brentwood, TN: Howard Books, 2013), 20.

15. McManus, *Soul Cravings,* 23.

16. *Barnes' Notes on Ephesians-Philemon* (Grand Rapids, MI: Baker Books, 1990), http://bibleapps com/commentaries/ephesians/4-29.htm

17. Dr. Larry Crabb, *66 Love Letters* (Nashville, TN: Thomas Nelson, 2009), 74.

18. Albert Barnes, *Notes, Explanatory and Practical, on the Epistles of Paul to the Ephesians, Philippians, and Colossians* (New York: Harper & Brothers, 1846), 116.

19. Brennan Manning, *The Ragamuffin Gospel* (Colorado Springs, CO: Multnomah, 2005), 106-107.

20. Dutch Sheets, *Roll Away Your Stone* (Bloomington, MN: Bethany House, 2007), 105.

21. C. S. Lewis, *The World's Last Night and Other Essays* (Mariner Book, 1 Edition, 2002), 109.

22. C. S. Lewis, *The Four Loves* (New York: Harcourt, Brace, 1960), 121.

23. Nicole Kear, "As the Lights Go Down," Southwest Airlines *Spirit* magazine, July 2014.

24. McManus, *Soul Cravings,* 8.

Other Books in the
Two Minutes in the Bible Series

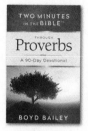

Two Minutes in the Bible Through Proverbs
To find practical answers for everyday challenges, you can't go wrong with the book of Proverbs. And to help you apply its timeless truth to every area of your own life, popular devotional writer Boyd Bailey offers these concise and down-to-earth daily readings.

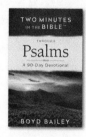

Two Minutes in the Bible Through Psalms
Raw. Real. Relevant. The psalms were written to lead you onward in your faith walk—deeper and closer to God's heart. Boyd Bailey of the Wisdom Hunters ministry takes a fresh look at the psalms in 90 thought-provoking devotions that draw you into the loving presence of the Lord.

Two Minutes in the Bible for Men
The answers to life's most important questions are found in Scripture and highlighted in these down-to-earth daily readings for men from Boyd Bailey. You'll find the wisdom and inspiration you need to grow in your personal character and connect with God in every area of your life.

To learn more about Harvest House books and
to read sample chapters, log on to our website:

www.harvesthousepublishers.com

HARVEST HOUSE PUBLISHERS
EUGENE, OREGON